HAUNTINGS

TRUE LIFE SIGHTINGS and EXPERIENCES OF GHOSTS

REBECCA E. KIDGER

WAVERLEY BOOKS

This edition published 2011 by Waverley Books,
144 Port Dundas Road,
Glasgow G4 0HZ

A catalogue entry for this book is available from the British Library.

ISBN 978-1-84934-069-4

Printed and bound in Europe

Contents

Introduction   9

Ghostly Grand Houses and Halls   12

RYECROFT HALL, LANCASHIRE   12
STANLEY PALACE, CHESTER   14
TISSINGTON HALL, DERBYSHIRE   16
HADDON HALL, DERBYSHIRE   17
CALKE ABBEY, DERBYSHIRE   19
HELLENS MANOR, HEREFORDSHIRE   20
HERGEST COURT, HEREFORDSHIRE   23
SOMERIES CASTLE, BEDFORDSHIRE   24
BROUGHAM HALL, CUMBRIA   26
ISEL HALL, CUMBRIA   27
WARDOWN PARK MUSEUM, LUTON   28
HANGLETON MANOR, EAST SUSSEX   31

Paranormal Public Houses and Inns

Paranormal Public Houses and Inns   34

THE WHITE HART INN, LEICESTERSHIRE   34
THE MINER'S ARMS, DERBYSHIRE   36
THE PIED BULL INN, LEICESTERSHIRE   37
THE LICHFIELD VAULTS, HEREFORD   38
THE OLD MANOR PUBLIC HOUSE, BERKSHIRE   39
THE BRICKLAYER'S ARMS, LUTON   40
THE MORPETH ARMS, MILLBANK, LONDON   43
THE HALFWAY HOUSE, CHESHIRE   44
THE STAG AND HOUND, BRISTOL   45
THE LLANDOGER TROW, BRISTOL   47
THE FOXHOUND PUB, BRIXTON   49
THE ANCIENT RAM INN, GLOUCESTERSHIRE   50
THE INN BURTLE, SOMERSET   52
THE GEORGE INN, DEVON   53
THE FLEECE INN, YORKSHIRE   55

Brutal Battlefields   59

FLODDEN, NORTHUMBERLAND   59
OTTERBURN, NORTHUMBERLAND   61
BOSWORTH FIELD, LEICESTERSHIRE   63
MARSTON MOOR, YORKSHIRE   64

Haunted Homes   66

A FAMILY HOME, COVENTRY   66
A PRIVATE RESIDENCE, NOTTINGHAMSHIRE   68
A FAMILY HOME, LEICESTERSHIRE   69
A COTTAGE, LEICESTERSHIRE   70
A VICTORIAN COTTAGE, LEICESTERSHIRE   71
A HOUSE, LEICESTERSHIRE   72
A FAMILY HOME, LEICESTERSHIRE   73

A Detached House, Leicestershire 74
A Private Residence, Northampton 75
A 17th-Century Cottage,
    Leicestershire 76
A Modern House, Cambridgeshire 78
A Family Home, Lancashire 79
A House in Wigan, Lancashire 81
A Family Home, Lancashire 83
A Three-Storey House, Manchester 85
A Private Residence, Torquay 85
A Seaside Residence, Plymouth 87
An Old House, Berkshire 88
A Basement Flat, London 91

Spirit-ridden Roads 92

Watergate Street, Chester 92
The M1, Nottinghamshire 93
A Country Lane, Leicestershire 94
A Road in Canewdon Village, Essex 95
Bartlett Street, Bath, Somerset 96
The Fosse Way 97

Spooky Shops 100

A Charity Shop, Warwickshire 100
A Hairdressing Salon, Lancashire 102
Bygone Times, Lancashire 103
The Best Little Hair House in Hereford 106

Wierd Workspaces 108

A Newspaper Office, Lancashire 108
A Warehouse, Nottinghamshire 110

Creepy Castles 111

THE TURRET GATEWAY, LEICESTER 111
ELVASTON CASTLE, HEREFORDSHIRE 113
GOODRICH CASTLE, HEREFORDSHIRE 113
DONNINGTON CASTLE, BERKSHIRE 114
DUNSTANBURGH CASTLE, NORTHUMBERLAND 116
CHILLINGHAM CASTLE, NORTHUMBERLAND 117
EDLINGHAM CASTLE, NORTHUMBRIA 119
CASTLE KEEP, NEWCASTLE UPON TYNE 122
SCARBOROUGH CASTLE, YORKSHIRE 123
WHORLTON CASTLE, YORKSHIRE 124
PENGERSICK CASTLE, CORNWALL 126
PENDENNIS CASTLE, CORNWALL 129

Petrifying Places of Worship 131

ST. MARY'S CHURCH, HEREFORDSHIRE 131
DERBY CATHEDRAL, DERBY 134
GRACEDIEU PRIORY, LEICESTERSHIRE 135
GODSTOW ABBEY, OXFORDSHIRE 136
THE CHURCH OF ST. MARY DE CASTRO,
  LEICESTER 137
LYDIATE ABBEY, MERSEYSIDE 139
EGGLESTONE ABBEY, COUNTY DURHAM 139
ST. CLETHER HOLY CHAPEL AND WELL,
  CORNWALL 141
WHITBY ABBEY, NORTH YORKSHIRE 142

Haunted Hotels 144

BESTWOOD LODGE, NOTTINGHAMSHIRE 144
THE CROWN AND THISTLE HOTEL,
  OXFORDSHIRE 145

The Feathers, Shropshire   146
Pengethley Manor, Herefordshire   149
The Green Dragon, Herefordshire   150
The Queens Hotel, Yorkshire   152
Arnos Manor Hotel, Bristol   153
Boringdon Hall, Plymouth   155
The Iron Duke Hotel, East Sussex   156
The Castle of Comfort Hotel, Somerset   158

Worrisome Wooded Areas   159

Hermit's Wood, Derbyshire   159
Charnwood Forest, Leicestershire   160
Wychwood Forest, Oxfordshire   161
Delamere Forest, Cheshire   163
Clapham Wood, West Sussex   163
Churston Woods, Devon   164

Petrifying Parkland   166

Bradgate Park, Leicestershire   166
St. James's Park, London   167

Watery Ends   169

Talkin Tarn, Cumbria   169
Slapton Sands   171

Eerie Entertainment Venues   172

A Cinema, London   172
The Gaumont Theatre, Liverpool   173
The Falstaff Experience,
  Stratford upon Avon   175

Ruined Roman Remains   177

CHESTER WALLS, CHESHIRE   177
CAWTHORN ROMAN CAMPS,
  NORTH YORKSHIRE   178
SILCHESTER ROMAN TOWN, HAMPSHIRE   179

A Mixture of Manifestations   181

COALHOUSE FORT, ESSEX   181
SELWYN HOUSE PREP SCHOOL, KENT   182
WINTER'S GIBBET, NORTHUMBERLAND   184
THE SPANISH BARN, TORQUAY   186
CRAG HALL MINE, YORKSHIRE   187
CALLOW HILL, HEREFORDSHIRE   187
ST. MARY'S GUILDHALL, WARWICKSHIRE   189

Acknowledgements   191

Introduction

England is a country with a rich history of pomp and pageantry, conflict and resolution, and from north to south it is filled with captivating scenery, impressive architecture and some of the most famous places in the world. It is also a country where ghosts are said to be lurking in many different locations, some famous, some not.

There is no doubt that from the dawn of time until today, people have been fascinated with the afterlife. Ghost stories are often part of local folklore with people passing down their tales from generation to generation through family and friends. They can be enchanting tales of times gone by brought to life because of a ghostly sighting or appearance, but they can also tell of terrifying and macabre events that vividly depict the gruesome side of human nature.

The presence of ghosts has been experienced by people throughout the land, with apparitions and manifestations being witnessed in a wide variety of locations, and a strong sense of paranormal activity exuding from others. Ghosts have captivated the imagination of people throughout the ages, fascinating minds because of the uncertainty of their existence and the mystery of their stories. Words such as 'the paranormal', 'spirits', 'manifestations' and 'apparitions' have become part of our everyday language.

This book delves into ghostly happenings in buildings and locations across the length and breadth of England. Sites of all ages are included – some from as long ago as Roman times right up to family homes built less than thirty years ago. There are tales of ghosts and ghouls, of pleasant spirits as well as perilous poltergeists, of people and all manner of creatures who are yet to rest in peace, dead but still trapped in eternal limbo in this world.

Many of the ghostly accounts within this book have been experienced and expressed to me by individuals keen to share their tales. From people who are part of paranormal organisations to people with no previous attachment to ghosts, all have wanted to pass on their encounters with the spirit world. Their stories will hopefully not only intrigue and entertain but also challenge the reader to think about the very existence of ghosts – a question yet to be truly answered.

The happenings in these stories cannot categorically be defined as true ghost sightings but rather it is for the you, the reader, to decide whether or not to believe in the events portrayed. The people who experienced the hauntings certainly have no doubts about what they heard and saw. After reading their stories, will you?

Ghostly Grand Houses and Halls

Of grand houses and halls in England there are plenty, but who or what lurks within is a mystery that enthrals ...

RYECROFT HALL, LANCASHIRE

The picturesque Grade-II listed property of Ryecroft Hall sits in beautiful green parkland in Audenshaw, Tameside. Although the hall does not look like a particularly frightening place from the outside, it is said that many spirits lurk within.

The land on which the hall stands was once owned by the 7th Earl of Stamford and Warrington. He sold the land in 1849 to a wealthy cotton-manufacturing family who had mills in Ryecroft. The head of the family, James Smith Buckley, built Ryecroft Hall on the land but when he died two years later the hall was still unfinished. In the sixty-four years that followed his death the hall was owned by four different Buckley family members before it was sold on to a man named Austin Hopkinson in 1913. An engineering entrepreneur with a factory in Audenshaw and later the MP for Mossley, Hopkinson bought the hall as a family home but during the First World War it was used as a Red Cross hospital, where injured soldiers were taken for treatment and to recuperate. In 1922 Hopkinson donated the hall and grounds to the people of Audenshaw and it is now home to Tameside Metropolitan Borough Council.

Within the Red Cross hospital, life would have been frantic, as doctors and nurses rushed around tending to the sick. It is quite possible that some of this past life continues within the building and the ghosts of some of its inhabitants are believed to still wander this Victorian mansion.

The presence of an angry lady has been noticed down in the cellar, where some believe the hospital mortuary may have been based while the hall was being run as a military hospital. In one of the rooms in the cellar, she is said to shout 'Get out!' at people. Some believe she was once a nurse who didn't want people to visit the mortuary. During the First World War and in order to keep morale high the general public were not allowed to know the extent of soldiers' injuries and deaths. So it is possible that she would have been in trouble if anyone had seen the bodies, and keeping people away is a duty she is still trying to carry out, even now.

On the door of the same room there is a sign that reads, 'Silence, Control Room', from the early days when the hall was used by the council. Perhaps sensitive information was kept in the room and this is the reason the angry woman's spirit is trying to keep people out.

Whatever her reason for shouting at unsuspecting visitors she is definitely trying to protect something or someone within the cellar room.

Other sightings in the hall include the ghost of an old caretaker lurking in the upstairs Gents toilet and the gentle spirit of a little girl floating around in the upper floors of the building.

Although Ryecroft Hall has only stood for about a hundred and sixty years, it has seen much of life's suffering and sadness behind its doors, so it comes as no surprise that the presence of paranormal activity is felt within the property.

STANLEY PALACE, CHESTER

Stanley Palace in Chester is known not only as a fine Grade II-listed Tudor building but also as one of Chester's most haunted buildings. Now owned by Chester City Council, it was built in 1591 for a man named Peter Warburton on or near to a medieval site that was once occupied by Dominican Friars.

There have been many subsequent owners down the years and the condition of the palace deteriorated until 1928 when it was handed over to the Chester City Council who have restored and extended the building. All these years of habitation could be why the palace has had such a large amount of paranormal activity witnessed and recorded in both photographs and on film.

The building itself is said to have a strange and very changeable atmosphere, possibly because of the plethora of spirits who are believed to dwell within its Tudor structure. The temperature is said to fluctuate heavily for no apparent reason, leading some to wonder if the spirits that roam freely around Stanley Palace are making their presences known at all times by controlling the heat in the house.

The paranormal activity has taken many forms, the most exciting of which are manifestations witnessed by people with their very own eyes: a former lady of the house has been seen by many and the rustling of her skirt has often been heard within the buiding; a male apparition has also been spotted, flamboyantly dressed in white and gold attire, and witnesses state that he stood for a few seconds before vanishing into thin air; one recorded incident of paranormal activity is that of a lady, possibly named Edie, who has been captured on camera sitting at a piano. Another event caught on video this time was the mesmerizing moment that a chair moved unaided across a room in the upstairs of the palace in the main gallery area.

The distressing vision of a little girl has also been seen lying on the stairs within Stanley Palace in a position that suggests she had just fallen down the stairs. Did she meet a tragic end on the stairs? Was this the very moment her spirit left her body and since that time has she been forever trapped within the palace? The witness to this apparition then watched as a mysterious blue light shot from the little girl up to ceiling before both light and girl disappeared.

The apparitions of animals have also been seen frequently throughout the property, generally in the form of three dogs and a black cat. The cat has been observed mainly in the stairs area where it continues to wander about Stanley Palace as it once did when alive.

Audible phenomena appear to be a common occurrence within the palace and a volunteer caretaker has remarked that he hears the haunting sounds of children playing and laughing within the building. He has also often heard the spooky sound of a lady singing. No doubt these sounds would send a shudder through anyone having the misfortune to hear them.

Doors are said to slam shut when no-one is near them and unexplained lights and mists are prevalent within the building. Eerily the distinctive fragrant scent of lavender has been smelled in Stanley Palace for no apparent reason. Could this be the favoured scent of one of the palace's sighted manifestations as she wafts down its hallways?

TISSINGTON HALL, DERBYSHIRE

In the beautiful Derbyshire countryside of the Peak District sits the Jacobean mansion of Tissington

Hall. The Tissington estate can be traced back to the Domesday Book, while the hall was built around 400 years ago on a site that has probably been inhabited since the Bronze Age. With such a long and ancient history, much of which has been shared with the FitzHerbert family, it should come as no surprise that Tissington Hall is said to be a hotbed of paranormal activity.

In its day the hall would have buzzed with the sound of servants and staff performing their daily duties for the FitzHerbert family. It is possible that some of them have never left the building where they once worked and it is their ghosts who haunt the corridors and rooms of the hall.

The paranormal activity witnessed at Tissington Hall has included floating light anomalies and creeping shadows as well as the frequent sound of creaking floorboards for which no living person is responsible. An unseen force has also been known to throw furniture around the rooms of the hall.

Whoever is the producer of the haunting happenings within the hall, they clearly wants their ghostly presence to be felt today.

HADDON HALL, BAKEWELL, DERBYSHIRE

Haddon Hall is an impressive fortified medieval manor house, nestling in the Peak District National

Park. Built by a man named Richard Vernon in 1170, it stands close to the quiet village of Bakewell, home to the famous pudding, but it is not the delicious aroma of Bakewell puddings baking in an oven that has drawn certain visitors to Haddon Hall but the ghostly beings that are said to haunt its buildings.

The hall has stood for over eight hundred years and in its lifetime it will undoubtedly have witnessed many events both joyous and sad. It is the less happy events which may explain the presence of a woman's ghost running down some steps as if she is being chased. This manifestation is said to have been seen by a number of people, deeply shocked at witnessing what might have been the final moments of the woman's life as she ran from her murderer.

There are also reports of other spirit sightings including that of a lonesome young boy, a monk in all his regalia and a mysterious blue woman.

According to some witnesses, numerous cold spots can be felt throughout the hall, which could be connected to the presence of the ghosts witnessed by its many visitors.

A walk around Haddon Hall may open your eyes to a little more than its history, indeed you could well come across one or two of its former residents!

Calke Abbey, Ticknall, Derbyshire

The Derbyshire countryside is known for its green rolling hills and beautiful views. However, it is also said to be home to some not so pleasant things.

The imposing Calke Abbey in the village of Ticknall, now a National Trust site, is the former home of the aristocratic Harpur-Crewe families who lived there for nearly three hundred and sixty years. Their baroque stately home never was an abbey although in the early 12th century the first buildings on the site belonged to a religious community.

Calke Abbey as it stands today was almost completely rebuilt at the beginning of the 18th century. It sits in 600 acres of parkland, now a National Nature Reserve, and has beautiful walled gardens, a restored Peach House and an ice-house. Although parts of Calke Abbey have fallen into disrepair, the idyllic setting of the former family home is welcoming and warm and attracts visitors from far and wide.

However, the interiors of the house and its buildings tell an altogether different story, for Calke Abbey is said to be home to a number of ghostly beings. Their presence has been felt both at night and during the day, a scary experience for anyone who until that moment had been unaware of their existence. Sightings of apparitions have taken the form of shadowy, mysterious figures wandering the halls and corridors of the partly derelict building.

The most common form of paranormal activity in

Calke Abbey is that of dramatic temperature changes and even at the height of summer the temperature has been known to plummet drastically for no obvious reason. The feeling of being watched has also been felt by visitors to the house but no-one has been able to find out who or what is responsible for these strange occurrences.

Some believe that the perpetrators could well be the spirits of servants of the family, forced for some reason into carrying out their former daily duties. Others think they are long-dead members of the family who are reluctant to leave their former home.

Although a shadow of its former self, Calke Abbey has a vast collection of treasures and curiosities and holds an important place in the history of Derbyshire. Ironically, the ghosts who are believed to haunt the house are maybe helping to bring this history vividly to life!

HELLENS MANOR, HEREFORDSHIRE

Just outside Hereford there is a small village named Much Marcle, where an old manor house stands proud. Hellens Manor dates back to the 11th century, when supposedly it was first occupied by French monks. In 1096, ownership was granted to the De Balun family, who were witnesses to the signing of the Magna Carta, and since then it has seen many owners. Descendants of Walter de Helyon, who gave the house its name, still live in Hellens Manor. It is now run by a family trust.

In the late 14th century the manor house was owned by Richard Walwyn, who made many changes to the property. In the stone hall within the manor much activity took place and from time to time it even took on the role of a court, where the Walwyns passed judgement on the accused from the gallery above the hall. In 1571 there was an earthquake that shook Hellens Manor to its core and caused lots of damage to the property. Sometime later Richard Walwyn became bankrupt and was forced to sell the manor to Fulke Walwyn, one of his relatives.

A tragic love story connected to Hellens Manor tells of a lady named Hetty Walwyn whose family lived in the manor house. Hetty fell in love with a man who was considered to be beneath her class. Her family were very ashamed of her, so she decided to leave Hellens Manor and marry her lover.

However, the long happy life that Hetty had dreamed of did not come about because when she was only twenty years old her husband died. Forced to move back to her family home to avoid destitution, Hetty's return to Hellens Manor was not welcomed by her family and the poor girl is believed to have been locked away in a room, where she remained until the day she died. It is believed that the only way she could communicate with the servants of the house and her family was by ringing a bell for attention.

Alone and upset, Hetty fell into a deep depression and was eventually driven mad by her confinement.

The day came when she could cope no more and she committed suicide.

Words written by Hetty during her more than thirty years of isolation and imprisonment can still be seen on the window of her old room in Hellens Manor, etched on the glass by her diamond ring. The words state: 'It is part of my virtue to abstain from what we love if it should prove our bain.'

Her ghost reputedly still haunts her former prison and the sad vision of her apparition has been seen a number of times around the property.

Many other spirits are said to reside at Hellens Manor, including the spirit of a priest in a room called Bloody Mary's room where he was reportedly slain by Parliamentarians during the Civil War. His ghostly presence as a figure in a dark hooded gown has been witnessed by people staying in the room.

During Victorian times, Hellens Manor was said to be so filled with paranormal occurrences that the servants of the family living there at the time refused to stay overnight in the house. Later, in the 1920s, even the owner moved out of the property after he kept being woken by the ghost of a family member.

With such a long and turbulent history, it should come as no surprise that Hellens Manor has witnessed such a lot of paranormal activity during the many centuries of its existence.

HERGEST COURT, HEREFORDSHIRE

Hergest Court in Kington near Hereford is an old stone and timber farmhouse, once the manor house of Hergest Estate in which it is situated. The estate dates back to the 13th century.

The building that stands today is said to be the setting of a truly chilling tale that could have well been the inspiration for Sir Arthur Conan Doyle's *The Hound of the Baskervilles*. It is said that Conan Doyle stayed at Hergest Court for a short time when it was owned by the Vaughan family, and the Baskerville family had a castle nearby in Eardisley. Some say that Conan Doyle was related to both the Vaughan family and the Baskervilles through marriage. It is the sinister stories of phantom black dogs, however, which are thought to have been his inspiration.

There have been many sightings of mysterious black dogs in Kington and the surrounding area but it is the chilling tale that originates in Hergest Court itself that is the most famous black dog ghost story. The tale goes that towards the end of the 15th century Hergest Court was inhabited by Sir Thomas Vaughan, who was known as Black Vaughan because of his cruelty. In 1469 during the War of the Roses, Black Vaughan was decapitated at the Battle of Banbury and it is said that his loyal dog, a huge black bloodhound, ran off with his master's bloodied head presumably with the intention of returning it to Hergest Court. The gory sight of the head itself has been spotted numerous times hovering around area close to Hergest Court while Black Vaughan and his dog have reportedly been seen together wandering in the direction of the local church.

Inside Hergest Court it is also said that the sound of a dog growling and barking and the patter of dog paws can sometimes be heard in the upstairs of the building.

Local legend predicts that if a person sees this demonic hound there will be a death in their family, and to this day many locals will not walk near Hergest Court after nightfall.

Someries Castle, Parish of Hyde, Bedfordshire

In 1430 a man named Sir John Wenlock began construction on what was to become his home in the Bedfordshire countryside. His red-brick building in the Parish of Hyde was one of the first brick buildings in England. Its name, Someries Castle, comes from an earlier Norman castle on the site, built by one William de Someries, but Wenlock's home was oddly named because it was in fact a fortified manor house and not a castle. Now a Scheduled Ancient Monument, the once grand building is no more. Only the gatehouse to the manor house remains standing and earthworks are all that is left of Wenlock's house and the original Norman castle.

Around this ancient site there is believed to be a plethora of paranormal activity, which has been witnessed by a number of different people.

Visitors are said to have experienced a very strong feeling that there are people present around the site even though there are no physical bodies to be seen. Frightening black figures and looming dark shapes and shadows, some no bigger than a domestic cat and others as big as a man, have been encountered all around the grounds of the old manor house, sending shivers of fear through the individuals who have witnessed them; a black figure approximately five feet tall has been seen standing in a doorway of the ruins; and the ghostly figure of a person has been witnessed walking in woods close to the site before vanishing.

Strangely a mysterious small red light has been seen on the ground below an archway in the ruins but no-one can discover what is causing this light anomaly.

Paranormal audio phenomena are also prevalent within the area: the sound of stone hitting stone in the ruins has been reported and it is thought that this noise is caused by mystical forces throwing stones at visitors to the ruins; an unusual clicking noise and loud thuds and bangs have also been heard as well as the sound of children's voices drifting in on the wind; rather scarily the haunting sound of a lady humming and a female voice calling the name 'Peter' have also been reported in the ruins.

With a site as old as Someries Castle, it seems safe to assume that at least some of its former inhabitants may have chosen to stay in this space for a long time after their deaths. Who they are and why they are there will probably always remain a mystery but people continue to walk around the ruins after dark searching for answers.

BROUGHAM HALL, CUMBRIA

Brougham Hall, near Penrith in Cumbria, has stood for 500 years and in the five centuries that life has pulsed through the hall, the place has seen many changes made to its structure both inside and out. Prior to Broughham Hall, a fortified manor is thought to have stood on the hilly site as early as 1307, meaning this area has been inhabited for over seven centuries.

Originally built by the de Burgham family, who were probably forerunners of the later Brougham family who owned the hall at different periods during its history, the hall that stands today was rescued from destruction in 1985. Work is ongoing on its external restoration and it is home to an array of arts and craft workshops and businesses.

Paranormal activity is said to be commonplace around the buildings of the hall and some visitors almost instantly experience a very scary feeling as they begin to explore the site. Shadowy spooky figures have been witnessed lurking in corners, ready to frighten anyone whose eyes happen to fall on them. People have reported feeling as though they have been touched by an invisible being, while others have told how they have heard breathing and murmuring in their ears coming from an unknown, unseen source.

There have been reports of mysterious tapping sounds being heard and orb phenomena have been photographed frequently within the hall. There are also areas within the old hall where people have experienced a sudden and unnatural drop in temperature.

It is not only people who have been affected by the suspected ghosts of Brougham Hall. Furniture has mystifyingly broken, with some items collapsing when no-one was near them, and people claim to have seen chairs falling to pieces and drawers opening unaided. Whoever the ghosts of Brougham Hall are, it would appear that they sometimes have poltergeist tendencies!

Isel Hall, Cockermouth, Cumbria

Privately owned, the grand Isel Hall in Cockermouth, Cumbria, has the reputation of being one of England's most haunted buildings. Situated at the top of a steep slope that leads down to the River Derwent, the house is surrounded by green fields and stunning views. One part of the house dates back to the Elizabethan era and the site has been occupied since Norman times. The building has stood through some of England's most tumultuous years, close as it is to the Scottish border.

Edward I (1239–1307), who was also known as the Hammer of the Scots, fought a brutal war against the Scots whose armies in turn made several forays into England. This resulted in small defensive towers known as Pele Towers being built to protect the local people and their animals in the event of a Scottish attack and there is one such tower attached to Isel Hall.

The hall has gained a reputation as a haunted building thanks to the many paranormal activities that are believed to have taken place within its walls: reputedly dark figures have been seen skulking inside and unexplained noises have been heard resonating from unknown sources.

The most famous ghost of Isel Hall is that of a woman wearing a blue gown, who has been seen at the end of men's beds in the dead of night. Obviously drawn to men rather than women, it is believed she means no harm but who she is remains a mystery. If encountered, this manifestation must be a haunting vison indeed.

Wardown Park Museum, Luton

Wardown Park Museum is part of Luton Culture and is within walking distance of the town centre of Luton. Situated in Wardown Park on the River Lea, the museum was once a grand Victorian house and it is said to contain a plethora of ghostly beings.

The house started out in the 1800s as a country

residence in a private estate owned by the How family. The building that stands today is a Victorian mansion that was largely rebuilt by a local solicitor on the site of the original house at a cost of some £10,000. The building has seen many different owners and has had some different uses over the years. During the First World War it was taken over as a military hospital. The park and its house were eventually donated to the people of Luton and restoration was completed in 2005.

The ghost of a former housekeeper is said to still reside in the mansion. One occasion on which her ghostly apparition was witnessed is reported to have happened in 1971 when two heating engineers were at work in the cellar of the old house: working late one night the two men heard the sound of footsteps coming down the cellar stairs towards them; both are said to have turned round to see before them the manifestation of a woman wearing a long dark dress with what appeared to be a bunch of keys on her belt.

Since this event the sound of footsteps with no apparent living source has often been heard both in the early morning and late at night on the stairs and around the building. Many have heard other audio paranormal phenomena in the former mansion, including the sinister noise of clunking chains. In the bar room, the spooky sound of someone saying 'Sssshhhhhhh!' as well as the sound of somebody clearing their throat and the clinking of glasses have also been heard.

On another occasion a spirit, thought to be the spirit

of a child due to its height, is said to have been captured going quickly past a CCTV monitor at the bottom of the stairs.

The manifestation of a lady with long flowing hair has also been seen in the building while in the tapestry room the figures of women and children, including the apparition of a little girl wearing a bonnet, have been witnessed. Did the little girl die within the walls of the building that she continues to grace today?

Perhaps because of the museum's days as a military hospital during the First World War, the presence of a soldier has been sighted walking back and forth in front of a medal display.

People have frequently experienced the feeling of someone standing behind them, with some claiming to have been touched on the arm by this invisible presence and others claiming that they have felt a pressure on their back, as if something or someone was pressing against them.

Another person is said to have suddenly experienced the unpleasant effects of a very severe headache that was accompanied by the feeling that their throat was blocked which made it hard for them to breathe properly, and all of this when they were apparently perfectly healthy only moments before.

Adding to such scary events, strange cold breezes have been felt within the walls of the building, particularly after darkness has fallen, and the smell of cigarette smoke has been noticed when nobody in the building has been smoking.

Unidentifiable white lights are said to have been

spotted whizzing around the interior of Wardown Museum, further heightening the prevalence of paranormal activity in the former family home.

On a trip to this particular Victorian mansion, you could well end up seeing more that just the Wardown Museum's artefacts and wares on display.

❧

HANGLETON MANOR, HOVE, EAST SUSSEX

When thinking about the coastal town of Hove in east Sussex (now part of the city of Brighton and Hove), the presence of ghosts would not be the first thing that springs to mind, but rather its seafront and beach which have become popular with visitors in recent years. However it has become clear that ghostly activity is bountiful within the area and Hangleton Manor is one of the places where these ghostly spirits are believed to be present.

Most of Hangleton Manor that stands today was built in the 1540s, however its buildings also consists of the Old Manor House, an older house that dates back to medieval times and is the oldest secular building in the Hove part of the city of Brighton and Hove. Hangleton Manor became the property of the army for a time during the Second World War before it was left in a state of near ruin in 1969.

Today Hangleton Manor and the Old Manor House are both Grade II-listed buildings that stand as a pub and restaurant complex in the ancient village of Hangleton, now a housing estate.

Hangleton Manor is noted as a place with lots of paranormal activity that has been documented on a huge scale. One such case of a ghostly sighting, is that of a 'brown silk dress' which has been reported to sweep through the hallways of the building and walk up the main staircase. Why this dress appears and who once wore it remain a mystery although some believe it might have been worn by Mrs Fiztherbert, the Prince Regent's lover in the 18th century, who is reputed to have visited Hangleton Manor during her lifetime.

Another ghostly account around the staircase tells of the manifestation of a pair of bodyless hands that have reputedly been seen floating above the staircase, while in the attic of the building the presence of a female has been reported in a sad and desperate state. Is this because of something which happened to her during her life? Something that led to her death? Or is it because she is still trapped, even in death, within Hangleton Manor? The spirit of a child is also said to be present in the attic with her. Some accounts of the manor's history state that an infant was thrown out of an attic window by its mother. Could this be the mother and her child within the attic still?

Former employees of Hangleton Manor have reported hearing a female phantom making weird rapping noises from behind wood panelling, as well as ghostly cries from a tortured soul. Could it be that one ghost, that of the woman in the attic, is producing all of the paranormal activity within Hangleton Manor, chilling the air and sending fear into anyone that experiences her otherworldly goings-on?

When raising your glass, be sure to toast the past ...

The White Hart Inn, Ashby de la Zouch, Leicestershire

The White Hart Inn is a pub in the Leicestershire medieval town of Ashby de la Zouch that is said to house many spirits of the dead. The White Hart has been a drinking establishment for over three hundred years and the inn is reputedly linked to Ashby Castle and a number of other buildings by a network of tunnels, which run under the town. In the past, the White Hart had close ties to Ashby Castle which once stood proudly in the town but now lies in ruins. The castle was built in the 12th century and after a long history it fell to Parliamentarian forces during the Civil War in 1646. The inn's cellars were once used as holding cells for prisoners awaiting punishment at the castle, many of whom would have been counting down the hours until their execution.

The White Hart was also used as a bear pit at one time but today it is not bears who send fear through some of its visitors but the plethora of paranormal activity that is associated with the building.

The ghosts of past residents of the inn and of the former prisoners who were housed in the depths of the building are known to have made their presences felt on a number of occasions. In the bar at the front of the inn, the spirit of a little girl named Mary is said to be present and the atmosphere within this particular area is known, on occasion, to feel quite uncomfortable. Paranormal flashes of lights have also been witnessed darting around this part of the White Hart.

Around the corridors within the inn many dark looming shadows have reputedly been seen moving around and sinister figures have been spotted standing in doorways, as if they are watching the inn's customers enjoying themselves. One in particular is said to be the apparition of a woman wearing a crinoline style dress with a shawl around her shoulders and it has been reported that one lady was suddenly so overcome with sadness on seeing this ghostly apparition that she burst into tears.

Undoubtedly the area within the White Hart that holds the most distressing history lies in the cellars where the old holding cells were situated. Dark shadows and figures of people have been spotted within this space and people claim to have been touched and had their hair pulled by a mysterious unseen being.

Objects housed within the area have also taken on lives of their own: barrels have been seen shaking violently; and during a paranormal investigation rather spookily a gas tap turned itself on, making a loud whoosh before suddenly turning itself off again.

The White Hart Inn certainly houses a plethora of beings from times long gone by, trapped within the walls where they were once lived, and more than likely spent, their final hours.

The Miner's Arms, Eyam, Derbyshire

Back in 1665, the village of Eyam in Derbyshire had the unfortunate fate of being ravaged by the bubonic plague or the Black Death as it was known. When the plague came to their village, the villagers decided to quarantine themselves within the village boundaries to stop the plague spreading. All of the families who lived there were affected and more than half of the village's residents fell victim to the disease and died.

The 17th-century Miner's Arms in Eyam was built just before the arrival of the Black Death. It is now an inn and restaurant and as with any building that has a long history it is said to be haunted.

Witnesses are said to have seen the ghostly figures of two women gliding around the inn, possibly victims of the Black Death – an experience that sent shivers down their spines. Others tell of doors opening and closing on their own, with no known human intervention, and of items going missing and turning up mysteriously in other parts of the building.

However the most memorable apparition to appear in the inn has been that of a woman dressed in black who has been seen on many occasions. Is she a long-dead victim of the 1665 plague who refuses to leave or is she a former resident of the Miner's Arms who for some reason is unable to pass from this life completely? Whoever the lady is, she has captivated the minds of visitors and local residents alike.

The Pied Bull Inn, Shepshed, Leicestershire

The Pied Bull Inn is a quaint, straw-thatched cottage-style pub in the town of Shepshed, once a centre for the wool trade. It is a popular drinking spot for many of the town's residents and people from the surrounding villages. The inn is over five hundred years old and has been a public house for most of that time. It has a large beer garden and many of its customers enjoy their English summer evenings with a pint in hand under its ornate thatched eaves.

A building as old at the Pied Bull cannot fail to

have held on to spirits from its past. From time to time people are said to feel cold spots in the inn and witnesses have seen what appeared to be the figure of a person walking past the door to the bar. They have also seen doors bang shut when there was no living person in the vicinity. Although the Pied Bull Inn is usually filled with noise and revellers, many are reticent to spend time alone there or to venture down into the cellar on their own, particularly after dark.

THE LICHFIELD VAULTS, HEREFORD

The Lichfield Vaults public house in Hereford welcomes anyone through its doors who wants to enjoy a drink, from visitors to the cathedral city to its local customers. The building in which the pub is housed has long been a drinking establishment but its name has changed a few times over the years since it was first mentioned as the Dog Inn in 1782. It appears to have had its present name, the Lichfield Vaults, from around 1880.

The pub is said to house paranormal activity on a considerable scale and has a resident ghost named George. There have been frequent occasions when the customers in the pub have seen spooky happenings. Objects have been moved about and some items have completely disappeared. Some customers are said to have witnessed bar mats flying about with such force that they have ended up metres away from where they started. Barrels in the cellar have been known to move around for no apparent reason. Paranormal activity witnessed within the pub has been seen during the day and at night.

Once a female member of staff was scarily locked in a store cupboard by an invisible being, and one of the pub's landladies was often pushed whilst standing behind the bar. One time she is also said to have watched a woman, who she presumed to be her cleaner, go into the Ladies toilet. She followed the woman into the toilet, only to find that there was no-one there. The cleaner was in fact in a different part of the pub altogether and had not been anywhere near the toilet at the time.

Many cold spots are felt in certain areas around the building that reputedly send a shiver down the spine of whoever walks through them. It would appear that not all of the paranormal activity is caused by George and it could well be that another spirit resides alongside him, causing havoc for the staff and customers of the Lichfield Vaults.

The Old Manor Public House, Berkshire

The Old Manor public house in Bracknell is a 17th-century brick manor house that is one of the oldest buildings in Bracknell. It was a private residence until the 1930s since when it has had a variety of different uses.

It is believed that the ghost of a hooded priest walks the corridors and rooms of the Old Manor pub. The priest is thought to have hidden here for some time when he was alive. Another apparition that reputedly visits the pub is the ghost of former customer, an old man named Burt, who has an easily recognisable handlebar moustache and a ruddy, red face.

Anyone going for a leisurely drink in the Old Manor public house may well get more than a pint and a packet of crisps at the bar – they could be sitting next to the spirit of a long-dead fellow-drinker!

The Bricklayer's Arms, Luton

The Bricklayer's Arms public house in Luton has been a drinking establishment for many years and it continues to give a warm welcome to its regulars and to any visiting customers who come inside to indulge in a pint or two. However, the pub is also home to a multitude of paranormal phenomena that have been experienced both in the light of day and in the dead of night.

Among the apparitions that have been witnessed in the pub, one in particular is of a tanned-looking man propping up the bar, with a wire-haired terrier by his side. Even though this punter is now in the afterlife it appears that he still wishes to visit the pub for a drink with his faithful companion.

Possibly the most frightening spooky happenings to take place in the pub are the endless amount of shadows and human-sized shapes that have frequently been seen creeping around and hiding in its dark corners.

Many flashing orbs and unusual light anomalies have also been spotted floating around the pub's interior, further adding to the presence of paranormal activity at the Bricklayer's Arms.

Audible phenomena are common in this pub with many unusual sounds heard and recorded from within its walls. Many different sounds have been heard by a variety of people visiting the pub: loud bangs and thuds have resonated around the interior and creaking has been heard in the bar area in places where no-one was standing; furniture in the pub has been known to sound as if it is moving across the floor, and in particular the sound of a chair scraping along the floor has been heard by some; the noise that a match makes when it is being struck has been experienced coming from an invisible being in the vicinity.

The terrifying sound of people talking and holding conversations has been picked up by psychically aware individuals. The voices of both men and women have been recorded onto audio equipment during paranormal investigations in the pub. One such recording was that of a woman who appeared to be moaning, possibly in physical or mental distress. Another is of a woman singing and practising her scales. People who have

41

heard this recording state that it sounds as if she is singing light opera. The haunting sound of a little girl crying has also been heard whilst some have had the frightening experience of hearing a man mumbling into their ears. All of these phenomena are sure to send shivers down the spines of anyone who comes into contact with them.

A common occurrence within the Bricklayer's Arms is the sound of mysterious footsteps reverberating around the building's rooms and corridors, leaving people with the feeling that an invisible person is walking right up to them. On one occasion some customers were standing near the cellar when they believe they heard someone walking up the cellar steps and slowly approaching them. However, nobody appeared as the footsteps grew closer and louder, leaving these individuals aghast.

People are said to have been physically touched whilst inside the old pub by some invisible force: some have expressed how they were touched on the arm and, rather frighteningly, one individual noted feeling that they had been hit on the back of the head so powerfully that they were on the verge of passing out.

People's belongings are also said to have been moved by an unknown entity. On one occasion, at the same time as a person's bag was mysteriously knocked off a table, a strange black shadow around 1.2 metres tall was seen moving away quickly. The spooky shape appeared to be running from one side of the room to the other. Was this a coincidence or not? Whoever the spirits are who instigate and carry out the paranormal phenomena in the Bricklayer's Arms, it is clear that they are intent on making people aware of their presence now and for a good while to come.

❦

THE MORPETH ARMS, MILLBANK, LONDON

The Morpeth Arms is a Grade II-listed building on the north bank of the River Thames that is said to house the spirits of many long-dead folk. The pub was built in 1845 to serve the wardens of the nearby Millbank Prison, on the site of which the Tate Gallery now stands. This notorious prison closed in 1890, but some of the prison cells that held people awaiting transportation to Australia still lie beneath the pub.

Conditions in Millbank Prison were harsh, with over a thousand prisoners incarcerated behind its walls. When the time came for the prisoners to leave for Australia, the convict ships would travel up the Thames and dock outside the prison, ready to be boarded. The deportees would then walk down a passageway that ran under the Morpeth Arms pub straight onto a ship that was ready to set sail for the other side of the world. Most deportees would never return to their homeland and many would never see their families again. Some of them would have committed serious crimes, such as murder, but others were banished from England for much lesser crimes.

The cells beneath the Morpeth Arms are said to

43

house the spirit of a convict who died shortly before he was due to be sent to Australia. Some believe he committed suicide rather than be sent to the other side of the world. Another apparition that haunts the pub is that of a man who escaped from the prison but tragically died in the tunnels beneath the pub as he could not get out. Whoever it is who haunts the pub, there's a good chance they experienced a tragic ending rather than be banished from their homeland.

Within the main bar area of the pub there are said to have been frightening occasions when customers have had their drinks knocked out of their hands and bottles have been smashed on the floor when no-one is anywhere near them.

The Morpeth Arms is a pleasant place to enjoy a tipple but you might end up sharing it with a new unseen friend.

The Halfway House, Cheshire

Childer Thornton, near Ellesmere Port in Cheshire, is home to a pub that is said to house a plethora of spooky entities that have shocked people to the core. The Halfway House pub was once a stagecoach stop between Chester and New Ferry in the 1770s. For hundreds of years weary travellers have pulled into the Halfway House for refreshment and rest before continuing on their way. But there are some, it is said, who for one reason or another have not moved on and their ghosts continue to grace the pub with their presence. Manifestations of both men and women spirits have been witnessed at this former stagecoach stop on the old Chester Road. One morning a visitor to the pub witnessed the apparition of a lady sitting on one of the benches in the pub. She looked about 80 years old and is said to have sighed heavily for some unknown reason.

As well as the figures of ghosts, visitors have also experienced the fixtures and fittings of the pub behaving oddly on occasions. The cigarette machine is noted as worryingly having a life of its own and the ash trays within the pub have mysteriously moved unaided.

It would appear that the unknown force behind these happenings has lived for a long time in the Halfway House pub and will continue to do so, worrying yet also intriguing the residents and regulars of the pub.

THE STAG AND HOUNDS, BRISTOL

The Stag and Hounds pub in Bristol is a known paranormal activity hot spot with many ghostly occurrences witnessed there over the years. A building has stood on the site of the pub since the 15th century but the structure of the building that stands today is mainly from the 18th century.

The Stag and Hounds pub is a Grade II-listed building with an interesting history. The site on which the pub stands was once used to hold an open-air court called a Pie-Poudre Court or Piepowders Court – a temporary court set up initially by the Normans to deal with travellers who had committed a crime while they were in the area to attend a local market or fair. At some stage the court reputedly moved into what is now the Stag and Hounds' upstairs function room.

Many dark shadows have been seen in the corridors and corners of the pub with dark entities lurking forebodingly in the shadows. A male presence wearing scruffy modern-day clothes has been sighted on an upstairs landing in the pub and the manifestation of a man dressed in clothes from the early 1900s and wearing a trilby hat has also been spotted wandering around. He has been seen walking through a wall in the cellar and this particular area is said to have a sad and somewhat depressing feel to it. People in the property next door have also witnessed a mysterious figure disappearing through walls in their building.

Numerous light anomalies have been spotted inside the pub and a large orb about the size of a football was witnessed floating around the main bar area. Some people have experienced an unexplainable heavy and weak feeling throughout their entire bodies when standing in the bar and on a few occasions glasses have been sent flying off tables onto the bar floor, as if being thrown by an invisible being.

Toilet doors in the pub have been known to open and close spookily on their own when not in use by any living person while disturbing knockings and worrying sounds on the stairs of the cellar have been heard with no obvious explanation for their occurrence.

Whoever is behind the paranormal activity within the Stag and Hounds clearly wants people to know that they are there and that they will not be leaving the building any time soon.

The Llandoger Trow, Bristol

An old pub in the city of Bristol, where the literary figure, Daniel Defoe, used to drink, the Llandoger Trow is said to house a plethora of ghostly beings.

Built in 1664, this pub has long had a connection with the docks and seafaring folk. During the 17th and 18th centuries it is believed that press gangs, forcefully recruiting for the Navy, were often active here, along with smugglers and vagabonds. The famous pirate Blackbeard may well have frequented the Llandoger Trow on occasion.

It is rumoured that it was here that Defoe met Alexander Selkirk on whom he based his book, *Robinson Crusoe*, and that the Llandoger Trow could well have been the inspiration for the Admiral Benbow, the pub in another of his books, *Treasure Island*.

The structure of the Tudor pub today has three cellars but it is believed that the Llandoger Trow used to have more cellars as well as a network of underground tunnels. These tunnels may well have been used by smugglers to hide and secretly transport their loot underneath the city.

As with any building that has seen many people through its doors, the Llandoger Trow is a place known to have plenty of paranormal goings-on. The ghost of a young boy with a limp, who lived and died at the pub, has been seen around the stairs. His name is believed to be Pierre and it is said he can be heard dragging his disabled leg along the floor.

On one occasion the figures of two men were recorded on the pub's CCTV cameras after it had closed for the night. Staff who were tidying the premises saw the two men and went to where they'd been seen to ask them to leave but to their amazement the men had unexplainably vanished into thin air.

On the stairs leading to the staff quarters in the pub, people get a general feeling of uneasiness and feel as if an unknown entity has brushed past them and in the staff quarters themselves some staff members have had the sensation of something or someone sitting at the end of their bed. Is this the spirit of somebody long-dead who once lived in the Llandoger Trow and continues to live there even in death?

In the pub restaurant, cutlery has been known to take on a life of its own and mysteriously move off tables.

In a room called the Jacobean Room, the temperature has been known to change dramatically in an instant and for no apparent reason, and icy cold spots have been experienced. Some people have felt a tingling in their bodies as if something has touched them, despite the fact that there is no-one else in the room; some have become aware of an oppressive atmosphere washing over them; and others feel as though their head is in a vice. Paranormal phenomena in the form of flashes of bright white light that appear from nowhere have also been witnessed in this room.

In another room, ominously called the Dead Cellar, perfectly healthy people have suddenly become breathless with a horrible tightness in their chests and a terrifying feeling of being watched is heightened by the notion that an unseen person is in the cellar with them.

Many orbs have been witnessed throughout the entire pub.

With such paranormal phenomena present within its walls the Llandoger Trow is certainly a pub where customers may well get more than they bargained for when ordering a drink at its bar.

THE FOXHOUND PUB, BRIXTON

The small village of Brixton near Plymouth has a pub that is said to be home to the ghosts of long-departed souls. People have felt the presences of a multitude of different spirits within the building, which has served as a public house since the late 18th century. It is believed that the property used to house a local Assizes room.

An overwhelming amount of visitors to the pub have

noted that they have felt like they were being watched by someone or something, even though they could not see the perpetrator. Many have also had the sensation of spirits rushing past them caused by feeling cold blasts of air on their bodies. In the back bar area of the pub a lady even experienced an unknown dark entity tugging at her hair – a terrifying experience that must have sent fear coursing through her entire body.

The Foxhound Pub would be a pleasant place for an evening drink but when darkness falls and the last orders are taken would you dare to wander its floors alone?

The Ancient Ram Inn, Gloucestershire

The former Ancient Ram Inn in Wotton-under-Edge, in Gloucestershire is no longer a pub but it is believed to be one of the most haunted buildings in England, with paranormal activity witnessed at a staggering level.

Built around 1145, the age of this Grade II-listed building could well be the reason for the plethora of ghostly beings that are thought to reside within its walls. It is said that the spot on which it now stands was once a pagan burial ground and rumours of devil worship abound. Linked to this is the possibility that the ritual sacrifice of children once took place there. Could some of these poor victims still wander this ancient space and could it be that these tragic souls have created some of the spooky goings-on that happen within the walls of the old building?

The inn itself has played host to many visitors over the years and during the late 13th century it welcomed the builders and masons working on the construction of the nearby St. Mary's Church. Is it these workers who have contributed to the many accounts of mysterious footsteps that have been heard around the old inn – some walking towards and even past people – with no sign of who or what is making them?

On one occasion visitors to the inn heard a loud bang coming from upstairs. Running up to see what had happened they found a picture on the floor at the top of the stairs in front of the honeymoon suite. The picture was of Edward VI and it appeared to have flown off the wall even though ordinarily it could not have fallen off unaided. It was as if someone had lifted the painting off the wall and thrown it to the ground. Who did this remains a mystery although they were clearly hoping to get attention and that they certainly achieved.

The honeymoon suite is reported to have experienced ghostly happenings on a grand scale. At times, it is said to turn extremely cold in there, so cold in fact that it takes a person's breath away. Strange emotions have also been felt in there, with people going from one end of the emotional scale to the other – one minute laughing uncontrollably, almost hysterically, and the next feeling extremely angry and sometimes light-headed.

In the aptly named Bishop's Room the apparition

of a priestly figure is said to have been seen on many occasions, and cold blasts of air have been felt around the room even when there has been a roaring fire in place. The room is also said to darken mysteriously at times as if something or someone is preparing to embark on some paranormal activity.

The Ancient Ram Inn has many random objects scattered around, somehow heightening the expectation that paranormal happenings are just waiting to happen. It is certainly a place that people enter wondering what, or even who, they are going to encounter inside.

THE INN BURTLE, SOMERSET

The old Inn Burtle that sits on the edge of Sedgemoor in Somerset was originally a cider house but now the 16th-century building is a pub and restaurant, welcoming visitors to the region from far and wide. It still makes its own cider from apples grown in an orchard behind the pub.

However, rather disturbingly, numerous strange spooky happenings are said to have befallen many who have entered the inn. Local paranormal investigators have held investigations within the building to try and find reasons for this paranormal activity.

There are said to be unexplainable temperature fluctuations inside the inn and in line with this some people have experienced a feeling that there is a fire burning somewhere within the building. Others have noted that their feet have become very hot. Although the date is unknown, the inn was once consumed by fire and this may be the reason that some people have been affected by these paranormal happenings involving fire and heat when they enter the inn.

On other occasions people say they have felt a hand being placed on their shoulder when walking around the property – a disturbing and unnerving experience for anyone.

One of the bedrooms in the inn is said to have a very depressing atmosphere and many who have been in this one particular room strongly believe that it is haunted by a mysterious male spirit.

The presence of another male ghost is often felt in the office, where cold blasts of air have been experienced by some people.

Who these spirits are and why they choose to live within the walls of the Inn Burtle is a mystery but paranormal investigators will continue to be drawn to this building in search of answers.

The George Inn, Blackawton, Devon

The George Inn has stood for many centuries in the small village of Blackawton in Devon. The original building on this site dated back to the 13th century but a fire destroyed the inn in 1948. Now fully renovated this traditional English pub resonates with paranormal activity including some terrifying poltergeist incidents that have been witnessed by many.

During its history, many famous people are thought to have graced the George Inn with their presence. It is told that after Sir Walter Raleigh married Elizabeth Throckmorton in the nearby local church they spent their first night as a married couple in what was then called the Church House Inn. Many years later it is rumoured that Oliver Cromwell lived at the inn for a short time, probably during the English Civil War when he frequently travelled the length and breadth of the country.

Poltergeist activity has been experienced throughout the building and in particular in the upstairs of the property. Here the sound of footsteps have been heard running down the corridors accompanied by loud knocks on each of the bedroom doors. This must cause the people sleeping there to wake with quite a fright!

There have been sightings of numerous apparitions inside the George Inn: a small smiling lady was witnessed in the bar area by a man who was hoovering and tidying up after closing time; a tall hunchbacked figure has been known to appear in the living area of the inn, being seen on one occasion next to the television; the hazy figures of two small children have been witnessed along with a mysterious hooded female figure; and the frightening sight of ghostly monks has been experienced by some. One tale is told of the spooky manifestations of three monk-like figures that were seen to walk through the wall in the living area and into the adjacent hallway where they subsequently disappeared.

Mysterious cold spots are often felt in the inn, leading people to question whether these are somehow connected to the apparitions seen throughout the building.

One of the strangest but not so scary paranormal events at the inn happened when the owner found some 2p coins scattered in his shower. How and why these have appeared is a mystery.

The George Inn is a place with lots of paranormal goings-on and a long history, making it a rather interesting and sometimes spooky place to visit. Who knows you may well end up sharing a pint with a poltergeist!

The Fleece Inn, Elland, Yorkshire

The Fleece Inn in the old town of Elland in Yorkshire is a building that reputedly houses spirits from many different centuries. It was built in the early 17th century and was originally a farmhouse known as Great House Farm.

The building has had a long history full of crime and

incident, with several murders taking place there over the centuries, and it is said that the ghosts of some of these tragic victims and their evil killers still haunt the Fleece Inn today.

The Fleece Inn once sold more than food and alcohol within its walls. It is believed that local prostitutes would often tout for customers in the pub, hoping that the ale would help the flow of their business. One such working girl, who was pregnant at the time of her death, is thought to have been murdered with an axe. In another incident a serving girl was brutally beaten and pushed down the stairs to her death and she is said to still dwell close to the spot where she died.

The most famous ghost associated with the Fleece Inn goes by the name of Leathery Coits. He is said to travel at great speed past the old Fleece Inn without his head and in a carriage drawn by headless horses.

Another story is told of a visitor to the Elland market at the beginning of the 19th century who was killed by a local man in the Fleece Inn after a fight broke out between the two men. The murdered man's blood-stained handprint on the stairs survived for about a hundred and sixty years despite many attempts to remove it but eventually it was destroyed during renovations to the inn in the 1970s.

Many other shadowy figures have been seen moving all around the Fleece Inn but along with the Fleece Inn's macabre and gruesome ghosts, there are reputedly many spirits who have made the inn their home having lived there happily while they were alive. From the time when the inn was a farmhouse, the ghost of a farmer named Will is said to sit in a chair by the fireplace. During his life he would no doubt have enjoyed coming in, taking off his boots and sitting there after a hard day's work out in the fields. His presence has been felt on a number of occasions. Two other spirits, Alice Pollard and William Wooler, who are believed to walk the floors of the Fleece Inn have strong connections with their present home – both were landlords in the 1800s.

Rather bizarrely the pleasing aroma of freshly baked bread has been noticed in the building in an area that is thought to have once been the kitchen, possibly back in the days before the building was converted into an inn. A lemony smell has also been experienced, arising quite suddenly and with no apparent source.

In the kitchen the apparition of a young girl is said to run through the room and up the stairs. Her name is thought to be Jessie and she has been heard giggling as she runs around the building.

Running footsteps and spooky voices are often heard in the upstairs of the building while a strange banging coming from an invisible source has been experienced throughout the old building.

At times the Fleece Inn is said to take on an oppressive atmosphere and some people have spoken about feeling extremely sad inside the building and wanting to burst into tears. Some have also had the uneasy feeling of being intoxicated even though they have consumed no alcohol. Undoubtedly many people would have been inebriated within the Fleece Inn over the years and unsuspecting visitors to the building today could well be absorbing this sensation from a ghost.

The Fleece Inn certainly seems to have housed a multitude of ghosts for many years, with many yet to pass over to the other side.

Brutal Battlefields

Where once the clash of swords and the screams of men were heard, it would seem there are some who may not have left the place of their death ...

THE BATTLE OF FLODDEN, NORTHUMBERLAND

On 9 September 1513, England witnessed one of the bloodiest battles ever to take place on its soil. The Battle of Flodden saw around 14,000 people lose their lives in the Northumberland fields as King James IV and his Scottish army crossed the border to invade England. They were met by an army headed by Thomas Howard, Earl of Surrey, determined not to let the Scots succeed. The two armies began the battle a mile apart, with Branxton Moor between them – the Scots positioned at Flodden Hill and the English on higher ground at Branxton.

They fought for hours through mist and rain with the Scots using 18-foot pikes as their main weapons and the English their shorter bills (hooked chopping blades mounted on a staff), longbows and cannon. The English strategy was far superior to that of the Scots and the Scottish forces were defeated with a huge loss of life. Apart from the thousands of ordinary soldiers that were killed during the battle, many Scottish noblemen including James IV himself, leaders of the Scottish church including the Archbishop of St. Andrews, and many Earls of Scotland also died.

Due to the immense loss of life on this battlefield it should come as no surprise that there is a great deal of paranormal activity in the area and the spirits of many soldiers are said to haunt the now peaceful farmland. Many of the dead are thought to have been buried in a deep pit somewhere in or very close to the battlefield, forever to lie in the place where they met their untimely and horrific ends. Others are believed to have been put in a pit in the churchyard in Branxton.

The paranormal activity has taken many different forms, each as frightening as the next!

The scary feeling of being followed by an invisible being has been experienced by many visitors to the battlefield.

There are frequent reports of the ghostly sounds of battle and of mysterious whispering coming from the hedgerows around the fields. Could these be the spirits of long-dead soldiers, still hiding safely out of harm's way? The distinctive sounds of swords clashing together and the screaming and groaning of dying soldiers have been heard coming from the former battlefield by many local people, particularly at night when all around is a little quieter.

There are many accounts of unsuspecting drivers travelling along the A697, near to the battlefield, who claim to have witnessed manifestations of soldiers crossing the road in front of them, dressed in the garb they would have worn in battle almost five hundred years before.

In the 1700s, two brothers claimed to have witnessed a re-enactment of the entire battle in this area. When questioned afterwards they could precisely recount what had happened during the battle some two hundred years before, what the people involved in the battle had looked like and even what was on their banners.

Modern battery-powered torches have been known to turn themselves on and off for no known reason, when people have used them to find their way around the battlefield at night. Photographs have shown unusual orb phenomena in the area.

The Flodden battlefield is certainly a place with a sad and gruesome history and with such a large loss of life it is no surprise that many of the spirits are believed to still reside on the spot where they met their maker.

The Battle of Otterburn, Northumberland

The Battle of Otterburn took place on a moonlit night

in 1388 between invading Scots from the north, under the leadership of the Earl of Douglas, and the English army of Henry Percy, 1st Earl of Northumberland, under his sons, Henry 'Hotspur' Percy and his brother. It was a short-lived battle, but the fallen were many on both sides. Soldiers young and old lost their lives in a battle which ended in victory for the Scots.

Since then many unexplainable paranormal occurrences have been experienced on the site of the battle. Ghostly beings are said to reside in, and still wander, the field where they were slain many centuries ago. Back in 1888 two men were going about their business around the battle area when they are said to have witnessed some mystifying events: they claim to have heard the sounds of a battle, trumpets braying, men screaming and shouting, the clash of armour and the hooves of horses galloping towards them; they also said they had seen an apparition of some cavalry on a ridge close to them with the men wearing what could only be described as 14th-century armour. Astounded by what they had seen the men climbed to the top of the hill and, while noises continued to resonate from the area and the shrill sound of death and anguish was clearly apparent, they watched a ghostly re-enactment of a battle right in front of their eyes.

Since then people have continued to see the imposing ghosts of soldiers around the battle area. Many visiting the monument to the battle have heard spooky footsteps while some claim to have been overwhelmed by a feeling of nausea.

With so many lives lost in this area of Otterburn

it is apparent that many of the souls of the dead still wander their old battleground, forever trapped where they took their last breath.

THE BATTLE OF BOSWORTH FIELD, LEICESTERSHIRE

The Battle of Bosworth Field was the last major battle in the the War of the Roses, the civil war waged across England in the 15th century between the House of Lancaster and the House of York. It was fought on 22 August 1485 in fields near to the Leicestershire village of Bosworth and won by the Lancastrians. Richard III the last Yorkist king was defeated by Henry Tudor, Earl of Richmond, who shortly became the first king of a Tudor dynasty that was to reign over England for more than a hundred years.

According to Shakespeare it was during the Battle of Bosworth Field that Richard III spoke the immortal words 'My horse, my horse, my kingdom for a horse' as his efforts to defend his crown came to a brutal end.

Although the exact location of the battlefield is disputed some people visiting the Bosworth Battlefield Heritage Centre and exploring the fields around there have noted feeling a strange, forboding presence that has made them question whether they were alone and this would suggest that the battle occurred somewhere in this area. Some have even claimed to have heard the sounds of a battle echoing around them, with the clash of swords and the shouts of men desperately fighting for king and country as well as their own lives. Over five hundred years ago, the groans and screams of dying men would surely have reverberated around the battlefield and beyond, travelling far and wide, over green rolling hills and beautiful countryside.

With tragedy and death on such a scale it seems more than conceivable that some of the residual energy left over from the battle still remains in the green English countryside that may once have borne witness to one of England's most famous battles.

THE BATTLE OF MARSTON MOOR, YORKSHIRE

On wild, rough moorland in Yorkshire a battle took place that was pivotal to the whole outcome of the English Civil War.

At dusk on 2 July 1644, the Royalists, led by Prince Rupert and the Marquess of Newcastle, fought a joint force of Parliamentarians and Scottish Covenanters led by Lord Fairfax and the Earl of Manchester.

It was late in the day and not expecting battle to commence until the next morning, the Royalists had relaxed their defences. The Scots and Parliamentarians launched a surprise attack and after two hours or so of bitter fighting, the Parliamentarian cavalry under

Oliver Cromwell routed the Royalist cavalry from the field and defeated the remaining Royalist infantry. Some 4,000 Royalists were slain during the battle while only 300 or so Parliamentarian soldiers died. Cromwell's reputation as a good leader and cavalry commander was firmly established after his part in this battle.

Almost four hundred years after Marston Moor, it is said that the noise of battle can still be heard resonating around the battlefield: some people have told of hearing the groans and screams of wounded, stricken men and the bloodcurdling sound of battle cries.

The apparitions of soldiers and horses have also been seen wandering in the area, sending a chill through anyone who witnesses their long-dead manifestations. Visitors to the battlefield have also noted feelings of anxiety and nervousness, which could be left over from the fear and emotional stress of men fighting for their lives during battle, no doubt petrified by what they were seeing before them and of what was about to happen to them.

As on any ancient battlefield, it can come as no surprise that some of the fallen are still wandering Marston Moor in death, as they once did in life.

Haunted Homes

A home should be a haven, a place to feel secure, where guests can be graciously welcomed. But in some homes there are uninvited guests who do not want to leave ...

A FAMILY HOME, COVENTRY

There is a family home in the city of Coventry that is believed to house the spirits of three individuals who have made their presence known through a variety of paranormal activities.

Banging sounds have been heard in the dead of night as well as footsteps pacing around in the upstairs of the house and there is no obvious source for either of these events. The furniture in the property has often taken on a life of its own with drawers and wardrobe doors opening and shutting unaided. Once this happened with such force that the household were woken by the noise. The family have also experienced the frightening sensation of being touched in the night by invisible hands and frequently have the feeling of being watched by unseen eyes in their own home.

Three ghosts are believed to dwell in the house: the ghost of a French woman from the 1930s who is said to have worked as a nanny in the area and the ghosts of two children who died in car crash near to the house.

These spirits are not believed to have had any connection to the house when they were alive but are thought to have been drawn to the spot after they died. The nanny is said to have worked in another house in the area but dying young and believing her life's work to be incomplete, it would appear that she decided to carry on caring for children in the spirit world.

She may have been attracted to this particular house because it was a pleasant family home, where the house owners and their children enjoy a happy and comfortable existence. Perhaps during her lifetime she had not experienced the pleasures of a happy home life herself and so was drawn to the building after her death.

It is thought that when the two children were killed locally in a car crash their spirits did not move on because they were lost and looking for their parents. Possibly they did not even realise that they had died. It is believed that the French nanny decided to take care of the children in the spirit world and so she welcomed them into the house that she had made her home.

All of the mysterious noises resonating around the house are believed to be her attempts to make herself and the ghostly children known to the family. She wants their help because she is desperate for her and the children to pass over and be at peace.

A Private Residence, Hucknall, Nottinghamshire

In the former mining town of Hucknall there is a detached house, built in the 1950s, that is said to house the spirit of a former resident who has never left his home even in death. He had lived in the house for many years with his wife and two daughters, but after he died, mysterious unexplainable things started to happen in the house that baffled his widow and her daughters.

During the spring after the man's death, one of his daughters was out pruning roses in the garden when all of a sudden she saw something that shocked her to the core. For when she looked up she saw an apparition of her father cycling straight towards her on his bicycle. Startled, she screamed and fell back into the garden. Her father had never had a car and had always ridden a bicycle wherever he went. His family even joked that he should have been buried with his bike as he was so attached to it.

One day while sitting in her house, the man's wife saw him standing in the room with her. She fiercely believes this was her husband's ghost and not just a product of her imagination. Another frequent and unusual occurrence in the house was that the smoke alarm would go off for absolutely no reason.

In the house there was an old, rusty, broken musical box belonging to the family which had not been opened for years, when, all of a sudden one day without anyone touching it and for no apparent reason, it suddenly started playing. The family were bemused as they had not heard it for years and up until that moment they had not been able to open it because rust had sealed it shut. Was this the ghost of the man trying to make his family aware of his presence?

All of the paranormal happenings that took place within the house have been put down to the husband and father who had lived and died there, and to this day his family still believe this to be true.

A FAMILY HOME, MELTON MOWBRAY, LEICESTERSHIRE

In the market town of Melton Mowbray, famous for its pork pies and Stilton cheese, there is a house, less than a hundred years old, that is said to be haunted by a spirit who tries to communicate with people in the dead of night. Built in the 1920s this family home has experienced paranormal activity that has got a little too close for comfort at times.

One night the elder daughter of the family was fast asleep in her bed when something whispered her name repeatedly into her ear, even though no-one was in the room with her. She awoke with a start, shot upright and bolted into her parents' bedroom, screaming and crying with fear. The girl was studying for her A-level exams so her parents presumed she had had a nightmare because of the stress she was under.

However, some time later her younger sister had the same experience except that she came face to face with the ghost that was speaking her name. She was asleep one night when, as with her older sister, something repeatedly whispered her name into her ear. She woke up and looked towards the end of her bed, where she saw the figure of a person sitting. Presuming it to be her younger brother, she asked him why he had woken her but the figure sat motionless on the bed until she put the light on at which point it vanished into thin air.

Could this apparition be that of a former resident of the family home, who still wants to live there and communicate with the young people of the family?

A Cottage, Leicestershire

There is an old cottage in a small quaint village in north-west Leicestershire, where haunting happenings have been experienced. The listed building with its exposed beams is said to hold the strong presence of a male spirit, who likes to play with women visitors to the house. The male owner of the house had never experienced anything untoward in the cottage until one day, as his cleaner was going about her duties and tidying up the house, a downstairs radiator started banging loudly. The cleaner ran downstairs to see what the commotion was only to find that the noise was very loud indeed, as if a huge lorry was driving by outside. A large low-hanging chandelier hanging in the same downstairs room was bizarrely swinging from side to side.

Some time later the cleaner told the owner of the house about these strange occurrences and intrigued he invited a medium around to see what he thought about the house. When the medium stepped into the room where all of the paranormal activity had taken place, he suddenly felt extremely unwell. He became very distressed and clutched his throat as if he was struggling to breathe. Becoming extremely agitated, he insisted on leaving the room.

The medium came to the following conclusions: the ghost was that of a man and the malevolent spirit that had caused him such distress was the spirit of the owner's uncle, who had hung himself in the property some years earlier.

A Victorian Cottage, Leicestershire

The friendly ghost of a former resident is said to haunt

a quaint Victorian cottage in the village of Barkby in Leicestershire. Witnesses have seen the figure of an old lady with a bun in her hair sitting downstairs beside the fire. One person who encountered this paranormal visitor was sleeping downstairs one night, when they awoke to see the apparition of the old lady poking at the fire. The sounds of a fire crackling accompanied this haunting vision, yet the person seeing the ghost was not at all frightened. It is thought that the ghostly lady has a friendly persona as she is said to smile at whoever sees her.

The name of this old lady is not known and why she chooses to sit by the fire is a mystery. However, it is more than likely that she lived in the cottage during her lifetime, possibly even dying there. She continues to grace a building in death that she most obviously loved in life.

A House, Scraptoft, Leicestershire

There is a house in the village of Scraptoft in Leicestershire where macabre and strange noises are often heard, sending a chill down the spine of anyone who experiences this paranormal activity.

The sound of chains clanking and being dragged downstairs in the house sends fear and dread through anyone who hears these awful sounds but no-one knows where these sinister noises come from or why they fill the house from time to time. It is even more curious that the sound of heavy chains should be heard in what is a relatively modern house.

On another occasion a guitar was heard being played despite the fact that there was no guitar in the house, let alone one being played by someone. Why this sound could be heard remains a mystery and continues to baffle witnesses of this paranormal event.

The same witnesses have also seen a drop-leaf table in the home moving strangely and shaking on its own. The catalyst for this occurrence is unknown.

Could it be that this apparent poltergeist activity is being carried out by the spirit of a former resident – unhappy perhaps about people living in its old home?

A Family Home, Shepshed, Leicestershire

In the small town of Shepshed in Leicestershire there are said to be a plethora of haunted buildings, one of which is a house that was only built in the latter part of the 20th century. It may seem strange to many that ghostly and otherworldly happenings should take place in a modern detached house of this period.

A young girl was the main witness to these strange occurrences. She is said to have spoken frequently to a mysterious dark figure in her bedroom. Her mother often heard her daughter chatting away to someone, but on entering the room she would find no-one there.

Now in her early twenties the girl has recently recounted what she witnessed all those years ago.

A Detached House, Shepshed, Leicestershire

Also in Shepshed, the owners of a detached house on a modern housing estate there have witnessed unexplainable phenomena from a time long before houses ever stood on the site. They are baffled as to why such happenings would occur in a three-bedroomed 1970s house in an area that has only ever been known as farmland.

One night a lady in the house was sitting in the comfort of the lounge watching television, when all of a sudden she was astonished to see a single black trouser leg walk past the glass lounge door. Startled, she jumped up and went to see who was walking by but to her shock there was no-one there – no living person that is.

Strange banging and tapping noises resonating from the ceiling have also been heard in the lounge when there was no-one present on the floor above. On occasion, the owners' dog looks up at the same ceiling and barks at thin air for no obvious reason. Could it be that this dog is seeing something within the walls of the home that is not visible to the human eye? It is well known that animals can pick up on ghostly presences, so is this what the family pet is doing?

On another occasion the same lady saw the haunting vision of a little girl wearing a lace dress walking past the glass lounge door, but once again only the bottom half of the girl was visible. As before she immediately went to investigate and as before no-one was there. The identity of the little girl remains a mystery but is it possible that long ago she once played there? We shall never know, but the family who live in the house today are intrigued as to what or who these apparitions could be that haunt their house.

A Private Residence, Northampton

There is a modern house in a quiet cul-de-sac in Northampton that is said to house spirits from a time long before the house was built. Ghostly beings have made their presences felt in unpleasant ways that have left the residents of the house scared to go to bed at night.

The paranormal phenomena have taken a variety of forms in the three-bedroom detached house, which was built on farmland back in the 1970s. Nothing in the history of this area provides a clue as to why the haunting happenings are taking place in the family home today.

The paranormal goings-on manifest in a variety of ways. Often they are present in an audible form, with loud unexplainable bangs being heard around the house but it is the ghostly activity that takes place when the people of the house are resting in bed that has scared them the most.

Sometimes it feels like the sheets on their beds are being moved or pulled by an invisible being and the floorboards in the bedrooms often creak as if someone is walking on them. On one occasion a girl was asleep in her bed with her foot hanging out over the side of the bed when it suddenly felt like an icy hand had grabbed her foot. Petrified, she woke instantly!

Whoever they are, the spirits residing in this family home are making their presence felt in some decidedly unpleasant ways.

A 17th-Century Cottage, Thringstone, Leicestershire

In the village of Thringstone in Leicestershire, there is a quaint white cottage built long ago in the 1620s. The property is the former gatehouse cottage to the Gracedieu Estate with a coach house and stables to the rear. From the outside, this cottage would seem like an idyllic place to call home but many who have stepped into the tiny cottage have come to form an altogether different opinion. Strange spooky experiences have instantly changed their minds with some people witnessing frightening paranormal activity throughout the home.

One such episode happened on a cold December night back in the 1990s when a man and a woman were visiting an elderly female relative who owned the cottage. While sitting by a roaring fire in the small lounge, both visitors suddenly felt a whoosh of cold air brush past their faces. Even though they were staunch sceptics of all things paranormal, they couldn't help but think instantly that this feeling was caused by the presence of a ghost. Although this took place on a winter's night, the cottage itself has often been noted for having a cold and solemn atmosphere even on the warmest summer's day and on entering it many experience a feeling of depression washing over them.

The upstairs of the cottage is a very spooky place with a permanent chill in the air. Strange shadows have been seen and people in the upstairs bedrooms have often heard the sound of creaking floorboards.

Downstairs in the cottage there is a large parlour. In the past, when people were so ill that it was thought they were going to die they were taken down from their bedroom to lie in a bed next to the ancient inglenook fireplace in the parlour below. This was for a practical reason: if a sick person died in their bed upstairs it was difficult to bring their body down the stairs of the cottage in a coffin as the stairs were so narrow and twisting.

A mirror used to be in place on the outside of the parlour door so that if the door was left ajar at an appropriate angle people sitting in the living area could keep an eye on the sick person in the parlour. A lot of people will have experienced their final hours of life in the parlour and their spirits could well still linger in the room; and many years after the last death it is said that parlour still has an odd somewhat heavy atmosphere, where the breathing of a perfectly healthy person can become quite laboured.

Some claim to have seen the figure of a man sitting in an old rocking-chair and a rather taller man wearing a long coat who appeared to be sporting long sideburns on his cheeks. It is not clear who these individuals are or what time they come from but they clearly have an attachment to the cottage that they are not yet ready to relinquish.

A Modern House, St Neots, Cambridgeshire

A family living in a house in the Cambridgeshire town of St. Neots are said to have experienced frightening paranormal events in their home for more than ten years.

Spooky apparitions have been witnessed around this modern property during the day and at night, scaring the owners and visitors to the house; the family pets have also been terrified by the strange dark figures creeping around the interior of their home. Even the electrics have been known to take on a life of their own.

It is believed that most of the unusual activity within the house is produced by the ghost of a man who drowned in a nearby river or canal. He likes to appear in front of the terrified owner of the house during the dead of night when all around is quiet. Once, as she lay sleeping in bed, he is said to have woken her and as her eyes opened she saw him standing there in a semi naked state. She described how he seemed to be bent over, looking extremely pale and strangely bloated and, most startling of all, with plants from a river bed hanging limply from his body.

People have frequently felt an oppressive atmosphere upstairs in the house and the presence of this tragic man's spirit is probably the reason why. He may well be looking for help and this is why he appears to people as a full apparition – not because he simply wants to frighten them.

A Family Home, Bolton, Lancashire

In a family home in Bolton the apparition of a child has been witnessed when darkness has fallen.

One night the dad of the family who lived in the house was fast asleep in bed when his young son came into the room and got into bed with him and his wife. This happened often as the young boy suffered from frequent nightmares. The dad got out of bed and went and got into his son's bed so they could all sleep a little more comfortably. As he got into the bed he lay on his side, but he felt uneasy as if someone was there and turned over to face the other way. To his amazement, there, standing by the bed was the figure of a child who had pulled a t-shirt up over his face, just as a footballer does when he has scored a goal.

Assuming the child was his son coming to get back into his own bed, the man asked the child a number of times if he was okay but got no reply. Bemused he then began to get out of bed, but as he did so the figure began to walk backwards away from him. Asking the child again what was wrong, he glanced down at the child's feet and noticed that the figure was not walking but was instead floating backwards towards the bedroom wall, through which it then disappeared.

Is it possible that this ghostly child had been visiting the son of the family often, causing the boy to believe he was having nightmares? Or was this a one-off visit from a child now residing in the afterlife? Since then the apparition has not been witnessed again but this haunting happening has certainly stayed with the family, for they sense that the apparition of the child could well re-appear at any time.

The house itself does not hold a bounty of other paranormal activity but the bottom of the stairs are said to be always freezing cold whatever the time of year and no matter how warm the rest of the house is. People also get the feeling that they do not want to dally on this spot and tend to rush over it. Whoever the young child was who visited the family home that night it would seem that he definitely has some form of attachment to the house.

A House in Wigan, Lancashire

The town of Wigan in Lancashire is famous for its rugby league tradition and much-mentioned pier. However, it is a family home in the town that has long intrigued local paranormal enthusiasts, as it is thought to house a troublesome poltergeist.

Paranormal activity on a grand scale was experienced in the house and the occurrences were so frightening and frequent that the family who lived there decided to move out and the house is currently up for sale.

Paranormal phenomena have taken the form of unexplainable loud bangs, doors closing of their own accord, the sound of foreboding footsteps and looming black shadows.

One of the strangest happenings in the house occurred when the people living there heard a loud bang from the living room and on entering the room found two fishing rods placed in the shape of the letter V on the floor. There was no-one in the room and no explanation as to how the fishing rods could have formed this shape unaided.

Another odd situation occurred when a mobile phone was heard ringing in the kitchen and then almost immediately found in pieces on the kitchen floor.

The most frightening ghostly happenings in the home involved apparitions which were seen on a number of occasions by different members of the family.

One night the lady of the house awoke to find a chilling black shadow standing by her bed. Her twelve-year-old son also witnessed a ghost but did not tell his parents. They only found out when, after a short while sleeping away from the family home at a relative's house, the boy said he did not want to return home because he was scared of the ghost in the house.

One night the father of the family happened to glance out of the window and witnessed a startling manifestation in the street outside his house. What he saw must surely have shocked and mystified him because standing there was a man and a woman in Victorian attire looking at each other. Amazed by what he was seeing he woke both his wife and son and they also saw this strange manifestation, but after that night none of them ever saw the Victorian couple again.

To have experienced paranormal activity on such a scale within a family home must surely have been terrifying for this family, so it comes as no surprise that they felt they could no longer live there. Hopefully the next family who reside within the house in Wigan do not experience such a plethora of paranormal activity.

A Family Home, Stalybridge, Lancashire

There is a house in the small town of Stalybridge in Lancashire, that bore witness to poltergeist activity so terrifying that after one particularly frightening episode the family who lived there moved out.

Paranormal activity was first witnessed one night when the man of the house was walking towards the kitchen and saw what he presumed was his step-son running into the spare bedroom. It was one o'clock in the morning so he wondered what the boy was up to. He ran upstairs intending to give the boy a telling off for playing around at such a late hour but on entering the spare room he was stunned to find that the boy was not there and the room stood empty.

This is not the only time when one person has been mistaken for another within this house. On another occasion the man's wife was asleep in bed when she was woken by someone she believed to be her husband getting into bed beside her. A short time later the lady got out of bed to go to the toilet and noticed that downstairs both the television and the living room light were still switched on. She returned to the bedroom all ready to tell her husband off for leaving everything turned on and wasting electricity but there was no sign of him in the bed or the room. In fact he was still sitting downstairs! It would appear that a ghost wanted to take the place of her husband.

Matters for the family really took a dramatic turn when they started to experience even more bizarre and frightening paranormal activity after buying a puppy.

For the first few weeks after its arrival the puppy was kept in a puppy pen in the kitchen at night. Banging and howling from the puppy would often be heard and first they presumed it was just the normal behaviour of a young puppy but one night the banging was so loud that it woke up the entire family.

Quite sure that their house was being broken into, the man of the house went downstairs with a cricket bat, ready to defend himself against the intruder. As he walked down the stairs, the light in the kitchen turned itself off which simply heightened his belief that he was being burgled and that an intruder awaited him beyond the door.

Furious, the man ran into the room bat in hand. Quickly turning the light back on he saw to his amazement there was no other human being present in the kitchen only the petrified puppy sitting in the middle of a cage that was being violently shaken by an unseen force. Scared beyond belief himself the man opened the cage door, grabbed the puppy and ran back upstairs to his wife.

After this terrifying event took place the dog never left his owners alone and they moved out of the house a few weeks later, too terrified to live there any longer.

The poltergeist activity witnessed within this family home would surely terrify even the most hardened person and moving out of the house was obviously the sensible thing to do.

A Three-Storey House, Hulme, Manchester

In the bustling city of Manchester many ghosts and ghouls roam the streets and buildings after dark, sending fear into whoever is unfortunate enough to cross their paths. This story focuses on a three-storey house built less than ten years ago that is thought to house the spirit of a long-dead soul.

The house is in the suburb of Hulme close to the city centre and for many years it has creaked and groaned with unusual noises that come from no apparent source. No-one is believed to have died there nor has there been any major tragedy on the spot where the house is built but, whatever the cause, these noises have worried residents into making sure that their bedrooms are securely locked when they go to sleep at night.

Objects are also known to mysteriously move to other areas of the house and paintings have fallen off walls, despite being securely hung and in position for a long time. It appears that whatever is instigating these unusual and frightening occurrences certainly has a bone to pick with this house in Hulme.

A Private Residence, Torquay

Torquay attracts thousands of tourists each year, all drawn to the bustling seaside town for entertainment and fun on the beach. However the town does not welcome visitors from this world only, for it is believed to house beings from an altogether different plane of existence. It is said that spirits roam freely in a mid-terraced property in the town, built in the early 1900s.

The family who currently live in the residence experience a plethora of unexplainable paranormal activity on an almost daily basis and fear what could happen next. Loud noises which take the form of knocking and rapping are often heard in the house, resonating from unknown sources. Objects are also moved about in the dead of night, disturbing and scaring the owners.

It is believed that one of the spirits who reside within this Torquay family home is that of an elderly man, who himself may have lived and died there. His spirit is said to be trapped within his former home but no-one knows why he refuses to leave. His footsteps are heard throughout the building on occasion and anyone hearing them feels instantly chilled to the bone. This gentleman may still believe the home to be his and is upset that other people now live there. His apparent behaviour from beyond the grave would certainly seem to confirm this.

The ghost of an elderly lady is also said to live within this mid-terraced house, but whether these two spirits are connected is a question yet to be answered.

A SEASIDE RESIDENCE, PLYMOUTH

The town of Plymouth has a long history of seafaring and continues to have strong maritime links but it is the resident ghosts at numerous locations around the city that are of interest to some people.

One particular terraced house in the old part of Plymouth is said to have experienced paranormal activity on a considerable scale. Separated into apartments, it is in one of these apartments that unexplainable occurrences are prevalent, often exacting poltergeist activity on the home owners.

A lady who lives there has been physically attacked by an unknown entity. Her hair was tugged and a door slammed violently into her arm, causing her to bruise badly. The spirit presumed to be responsible for these attacks is possibly that of a male who has an issue with females but we may never know for sure why he behaves like this.

The telephone has also been known to ring for no apparent reason even when the line is in use on the other handset. The television has been said to take on a strange blue glow even when it is switched off. Mysterious lights have been seen by the people who live there, whizzing around the rooms. With no apparent source for these lights, one thing witnesses are certain of is that they do not come from an electrical source. Some people have suggested that they could be the product of ghosts encircling the property they once lived in.

Music has also been known to play on the stereo

system in the apartment even though no-one has switched it on, and the volume also alters. Taps have been known to turn themselves on and off and doors are reported to frequently open and close on their own. On one sinister occasion the bathroom door is said to have been taken off its hinges!

Other spooky happenings that have taken place in this particular apartment in the old house in Plymouth are loud unexplainable banging and dramatic drops in temperature. A strong smell of tobacco has been noticed even though no-one has been smoking within the home.

The owner of the apartment tells of being tapped on the shoulder by a mysterious entity and of seeing the apparition of a child out of the corner of his eye. Another member of the household witnessed what they thought to be the figure of a small man standing in the doorway eerily looking right back at them.

Whoever these reported apparitions are, it is clear they still think of the apartment in Plymouth as their home.

An Old House, Near Pangbourne, Reading, Berkshire

Down a quiet, meandering track in a village near Pangbourne there is an old house that is said to contain spirits of the dead. The property is approximately 500 years old and was originally three separate cottages that were later converted into one house.

A family, that lived in the property from the mid-1950s to the 1970s experienced what can only be described as paranormal activity on a gargantuan scale.

One such episode happened not long after the family had moved into the house, when the mother and her friend were witnesses to a spooky happening that they will never forget. The two ladies were having a break from decorating an upstairs bedroom, when all of a sudden there was an enormous crash, which sounded as if the paint pots had been knocked over. Startled the two ladies ran upstairs to see what had happened, only to find everything as they had left it – not one object had been moved or disturbed.

The wooden staircase of the property was said to be the site of many unexplainable paranormal happenings, including the creaking sound of wooden floorboards as if someone was walking upstairs when in reality no-one was there. The family dogs would often spring to attention and bark for no obvious reason. Could it be that they were seeing something the humans in the house could not?

It is said that Oliver Cromwell stayed at the property after a battle near the house during the Civil War. History has it that he kept his horses in what became the family's dining room and apparently on warm summer days the smell of horses and stables was overwhelming in this room.

When the family lived in the property, the front of the house had a gravel drive and when cars pulled up to the house the gravel would make a crunching noise. On some baffling occasions, for apparently no reason, the gravel would make this sound as if vehicles were driving over it but on inspection no person or objects were found to be there.

Another spooky happening occurred on a dark winter's night when the mother of the house saw lights approaching the house from the main road. She presumed it was her husband returning home but as the vehicle drew closer it soon became clear that it was not the lights of a car that were shining bright but the lanterns of a horse-drawn carriage; to her amazement the carriage was not being pulled by horses but by the time she had moved to another window to get a better look the carriage had totally vanished.

On many occasions at the family home there was a knock on the front door at midday or at midnight but when the door was opened there was never anyone there. This happened many times and the family found out from previous owners that this also used to happen when they lived there.

With so many different paranormal experiences witnessed within and around the house, it is apparent that this space teems with ghosts but, thankfully for its current residents, none of them are of the unfriendly variety.

A Basement Flat, St. John's Wood, London

In a basement flat in a north London suburb, a strange paranormal occurrence has been reported. Although it has never been seen, the mysterious ghostly happening has often been experienced.

In the flat there are a pair of French windows that open onto a small garden and on a few occasions, even though these windows were shut, the occupant of the flat would get the feeling that someone or something was rushing in through them. Bizarrely he would wake up just before this strange event would take place and would instantly know it was going to happen. Awake and poised he would wait until all of a sudden it was as if an invisible dog bounded in through the French windows and jumped up onto his bed.

Although no image ever accompanied this occurrence it is clear that something was causing this phenomenon to happen. Was it the spirit of a dog who used to live in the building? Or is it the spirit of someone else manifesting in an unusual way?

Spirit-ridden Roads

We use them to get from A to B, but do you ever wonder what else travels along them that we cannot see …?

WATERGATE STREET, CHESTER

There is a street within historical Chester that is full of paranormal activity and many individuals have witnessed it at work. Apparitions of sailors and monks have been frequently spotted in the area, sending fear but also intrigue into the minds of the witnesses.

Some years ago at around 12.30 am in the area of Watergate Street, the apparition of a little girl was seen dressed in clothes from the 1970s. She was standing by the side of the road, solemnly swinging her arms and shuffling about on the spot. As well as clothes from the 1970s, she wore large glasses and had dark black hair and when the witness looked more closely at the girl's face he noticed that she had extremely dark eyes. Eyes in fact that looked almost like black holes. Frightened by what he had seen, the man reported the incident to the police, only to find out that such events were quite common – other people had also seen the little girl on different occasions. The location where she is seen is near to an old hospital and is known as an accident black spot which leads to the possibility that she could well have died here, or nearby.

The M1, Nottinghamshire

One night back in the 1970s, a couple were travelling southbound in the middle lane of the M1 motorway, between junctions 26 and 25. Driving home around midnight, after visiting friends, it seemed like any other car journey to the couple until one frightening moment they will never forget.

The motorway was not illuminated as it is today so the route was very dark and there were no other cars in sight. All of a sudden a man appeared in the car's headlights walking southwards just in front of them. The lady in the car screamed as did her husband as he slammed on the brakes and the car came to a stop. They were both badly shaken, thinking that they must have hit the man, but when they looked around for him they were even more shocked to find that he had completely disappeared. They had been travelling at 70 mph so would certainly have hit him if he had been a living person.

The apparition they had witnessed that night was of a man in his twenties, with dark hair, wearing a beige trench coat. Why this manifestation was walking down the middle lane of the southbound M1 is a mystery, but one thing is certain – he could well appear again on any given night around midnight.

A Country Lane just outside Belton, Leicestershire

One cold winter's night in the 1980s a husband and wife were out walking their dog on a quiet country lane just outside the small, picturesque village of Belton in Leicestershire. That night the lane was virtually pitch black and it was raining slightly. The only lights were coming from a farmhouse in the distance and car lights far away on the main road. As the couple walked around a bend in the road they witnessed something that they continue to talk about and that still baffles them to this day.

They believe they saw a ghostly apparition which presented as a white glowing shape with the build of a man, gliding along the road up ahead. The couple stopped in their tracks and watched as the manifestation suddenly vanished before their very eyes. Baffled and somewhat scared by what they had just witnessed they quickly made their way back to the comfort and warmth of their nearby home.

A Road in Canewdon Village, Essex

The remote Essex Marshland known as the Rochford Hundred is notorious for its connection to witchcraft over the centuries.

Two famous male witches from the area are James Murrell from Hadleigh and George Pickingill from Canewdon. In Essex, male witches were known as 'Cunning Men' and Murrell is often referred to as 'Cunning Murrell'. He is said to have precisely predicted the date and hour of his own death.

In Canewdon, George Pickingill lived rent free in a cottage by the Anchor Inn and was feared by many in the locality. He used his apparent skills in witchcraft to remove curses placed on farm animals and people, but in turn he would put many of his own curses on them and others. It is reported that people would know he was near them by the foul stench coming from his pipe.

Pickingill died in 1909 and there have been a few incidents when his ghost has been witnessed frighteningly up close. One night a man was driving from Wallasea Bay on the banks of the River Crouch and as he drove into the village of Canewdon he began to smell strong smoke coming from a pipe. He glanced in his mirror and saw the terrifying apparition of an old man sitting on the back seat. Despite being very shocked, he carried on driving and once he had left the village the vision of the man simply disappeared.

The apparition is believed to be the ghost of George Pickingill. The same thing happened to another man as he drove through the village. Why exactly Pickingill should need a lift around the village is not known but could he still be trying to cause disruption in Canewdon over a hundred years after his death?

Bartlett Street, Bath, Somerset

The spa town of Bath is renowned for its Georgian architecture, historical buildings and natural hot water springs. Jane Austen liked the city so much that she set up home there for some years. However, as night-time looms it is not only tourists but also some long-dead fellows who walk the streets of Bath.

Bartlett Street, in the Roman spa town, has a history of spooky sightings and one such event took place on a late autumn evening, back in the 1970s. A local hairstylist had closed up for the night at his premises in Broad Street and was walking to his car in a nearby car park at around 6 pm, just as he did every night after work. He crossed over to Bennet Street, a narrow lane that was used in the 18th century for sedan chairs, and from there into Wood Street. He recounts how he looked up to the right and startled saw what he thought at the time to be a gentleman in fancy dress. The figure was wearing long knee-length pointy black boots, a pair of baggy trousers, a black cape and a pointed broad-brimmed hat.

However, what followed made the hairstylist realise that the gentleman he was looking at was not a partygoer or an actor. For the apparition walked down the road and straight into a wall on Bartlett Street and disappeared before his eyes. Astonished and intrigued by what he had witnessed, the following day he returned to the wall expecting to see a hole where the man had disappeared. To his astonishment there was no hole to be seen – just a solid brick wall. He also recounts how cold this spot was compared to the rest of the surrounding area.

Whoever the apparition of the man in the fancy costume is, it seems for some reason he continues to walk the streets of Bath as he would have done when alive, even with a brick wall standing in his way.

THE FOSSE WAY

Julius Caesar sent the first significant Roman force to England in 55 BC but it was not until almost a century later, in AD 43, that the Roman occupation of the country they named Britannia began. After settling in England they set to work on constructing a network of straight roads that sliced through the countryside and linked settlements to one another. One of the principle roads that they created was the Fosse Way, which stretched from Lincolnshire right down to Exeter in the west country. Today the route taken by the road passes through cities, towns and countryside as it makes its way southwards.

The word Fosse is Latin in origin and means a 'ditch' and because of the name the road was given it is possible that it was originally a Roman defensive ditch marking the western frontier of Roman rule in Iron Age Britain. It may have been turned into a road later. There is also the possibility that a defensive ditch could well have run alongside the Fosse Way. Whatever its intended purpose, some 2,000 years after it was first built the road forms an integral part of the current modern road network.

At spots up and down the length of the Fosse Way people travelling along the road during the day and at night have witnessed sights that have startled them. It is said that many people have witnessed the manifestation of an entire Roman legion marching along the Fosse Way, just as they would have done many centuries ago. A Roman legion would have been an impressive but frightening sight to behold in the early days of the Roman occupation of England. Each Roman legionnaire was a fighting machine, decked in armour and carrying a shield and a sword wherever he went. Many never had a home or a family to return to and after joining up would have gone on to die in battle.

Strangely it is said that in visions of the Roman legionnaires that have been seen along the Fosse Way they are said to look as though they are walking on their knees, but this could well be because they were walking along the original road, now lying buried approximately a foot below today's road.

Spooky Shops

We go to a shop to purchase an item but some customers could come away with more than they bargained for ...

A Charity Shop, Bedworth, Warwickshire

In the market town of Bedworth in the West Midlands there is a shop where ghostly goings-on have been witnessed on a dramatic scale. The charity shop is believed to house the spirits of five people – two men and three children. It is thought that the shop was built on top of part of a graveyard and it could well be that the bodies of these spirits were disturbed when the shopping area was built.

The activity produced by the shop's ghosts has been so alarming that the number of people through its doors has declined and the shop has experienced a huge drop in sales as a result.

The strange happenings have taken a variety of forms: items in the shop have been moved and even thrown across the premises by unknown perpetrators; a table in the back office was scratched during the night and this was noticed instantly when the staff came in the next morning; dark shadows have frequently been seen creeping around the back of the shop, as if they are waiting to make their next move and find another way of disrupting business; and rather disturbingly, some of the shop's staff have occasionally felt ill for no reason, with feelings of nausea and dizziness commonly experienced.

The most prominent and it would appear friendly spirit in the charity shop is that of a man named George who is thought to have owned a local shoe shop. It is thought that he is the ghost who is moving the shop's wares around because he did not like how they were being displayed. It would appear that George just wanted to help out.

The three spirits of the children residing in the charity shop are thought to have the names of Geoff, Henrietta and Jessie. It is believed that they may all have died from carbon monoxide poisoning from a faulty gas fire whilst living near the shop. This could explain why members of staff have experienced feeling ill – perhaps they are feeling the ill effects of carbon monoxide poisoning, as felt by the children when they died? The scratch to the table has been put down to one of the children, who it would appear merely wanted something to draw on.

The fifth spirit, named Fred, is thought to be the ghost who is deterring people from buying anything in the shop by providing the establishment with an uncomfortable atmosphere. It is also thought to be his shadowy figure that has been spotted the most by staff members in the shop. Fred is believed to be a rather unhappy soul, due to his body being disturbed during the construction of the shopping area where the charity shop now stands. It is thought that his corpse may have been moved to another site and was not given a religious burial. Perhaps it is this that has upset him so much and that is why he haunts the area?

George and his fellow spirits at the charity shop appeared to have chosen to haunt this space because of the building's locality. Whether that is because they lived and worked in the area or were buried there does not matter. All that truly matters is that they were drawn to the shop and since that time have seen it as their home.

A HAIRDRESSING SALON, RIBBLE VALLEY, LANCASHIRE

There is a hairdressing salon in rural Lancashire that is said to welcome more than just living people through its doors for a cut and blow dry. The Grade II-listed building in the Ribble Valley is reputedly a hotbed of paranormal activity, where many of the happenings have scared people to the core.

Some of the mysterious events that have taken place in the building could be due to the fact that the premises were once used as a doctor's surgery. Unwell people would have visited the surgery in the hope of getting better but perhaps some did not leave and still haunt the building to this day?

Rather disturbingly a recording that was made when the hairdresser's was visited by paranormal investigators has revealed something alarming. When played back the sinister sentence 'There has been a murder here' is spoken by an unknown person. It is not known who spoke these terrifying words nor when the suspected murder is believed to have taken place.

Footsteps and loud unexplainable bangs have reverberated around the hairdressing salon. Sudden temperature drops have been felt and noted frequently and on one occasion a room went dramatically cold in an instant. The temperature is said to have dropped drastically by seven degrees. Light anomalies and orbs have also been witnessed around the building, further heightening the prevalence of paranormal activity within the hairdressing salon.

BYGONE TIMES, ECCLESTON, LANCASHIRE

Bygone Times is an antique lover's dream, an emporium full of antiques, collectables, curios, memorabilia and nostalgia based in Grove Mill, an old mill in Ecclestone near Chorley. The mill has been a place of much human and industrial activity for over four hundred years due to its position near to the Syd and Pye Brooks, both of which flow into the River Yarrow. In the 17th century it saw life as both a corn mill and a weaving mill and it also had close links to the English Civil War, when an army of almost 2,000 Parliamentarians used the nearby Eccleston Green as a temporary encampment after the Siege of Lathom House.

The long life that the Grove Mill site has experienced seems to have had an effect on the buildings that stand today. Bygone Times itself appears to hold the spirits of some who have been part of the site's long history. A plethora of paranormal activity has been experienced around this space and the site has come to have quite a reputation because of its many ghostly inhabitants.

The apparition of a monk has been spotted in the mill. He is believed to have a connection to medieval times and the nearby Park Hall, which was once a monastery, but now it seems that he likes wandering about in the vicinity of Bygone Times. Another apparition is thought to be the ghost of a young woman named Abigail who was murdered during the early 16th century.

The eery sound of galloping horses has often been heard near Syd Brook along with the haunting voices of the dead. It has been said that these paranormal phenomena are connected to the time when the site was an army base during the Civil War. The apparition of a Cavalier-type figure who wears a red jacket has also been witnessed wandering around what was once the shop floor of Grove Mill.

It is reported that the Grove Mill site once experienced a large explosion when some soldiers were mixing gunpowder for army supplies. Two men are believed to have died during this incident and it is possible that these tragic soldier's ghosts have never left the area and create some of the paranormal activity that occurs in this place.

The ghost of a young stable boy named Jacob has also been felt here. He is believed to have lived during the 18th century and it is thought that he was murdered by a horrible blacksmith for whom he worked Some think Jacob's life came to a premature end because of a blow to the head from the hand of the evil blacksmith. People have also experienced the feeling of something brushing against their legs in Bygone Times and it is thought that this is the ghost of the blacksmith's dog running excitedly around the visitors to the mill today.

Weaving mills were a place of work for children as well as adults. Thousands of children were unfortunate enough to have to begin their young working lives this way and it is said there are a multitude of children's ghosts still living at the Grove Mill site. Some have been felt within Bygone Times and their apparitions have been sighted in the cobbled alleyway at the old mill. The spirits of two young friends are thought to reside in this spot – a girl named Martha Wrennell searching the cobbled street for her friend Mary Ann Baybutt.

One of the most bizarre spirits said to haunt Bygone Times is that of a clown who wears a woollen hat. He has been spotted around the building and it is his spirit who is thought to prod people in the back to make them aware of his presence.

Another strange event took place some time ago when a man servicing a machine in the penny arcade at Bygone Times witnessed a rather bemusing incident. On emptying the machine of coins, one of the pennies disappeared into the ground before his eyes.

On another occasion when a man was painting part of the old mill at night he turned around to see what he thought was a real person walking towards him. The figure was dressed in a suit and on realising that his vision was not that of a living being the man became so frightened that he ran out of the building and never returned to finish his work.

It is thought that more than fifty ghosts haunt Bygone Times, making it a very interesting place to visit, particularly after dark.

THE BEST LITTLE HAIR HOUSE IN HEREFORD

When thinking of a location where ghosts dwell, it is fair to assume that a hairdressing salon would not be the first place that would instantly spring to mind. However, visit the Best Little Hair House in Hereford and this could all change, for it is said to be a building filled with poltergeist activity.

The exact number of spirit dwellers is not known, but however many there are they are sure to come from different periods of history.

Both staff and customers alike have heard unexplainable loud bangs, doors slamming shut and mysterious footsteps from all areas of the salon. A piece of wood has been thrown at a member of staff and there have also been incidents of flying pottery. When using the old staff room at the hairdresser's, staff have witnessed unexplainable bright lights. Cigar smoke can often be smelled down in the basement of the salon and a spine-chilling growl can sometimes be heard. Many members of staff over the years have been fearful to venture downstairs on their own.

The most disturbing incident of all at the shop was discovered by the staff when opening up early one morning. On reaching the salon they found that the reception windows were all steamed up from the inside and handprints adorned the inside of the windows. It is unclear how the windows came to be like this as the heating was never left on overnight in the salon.

Weird Workspaces

A place to work rather than play, but something is happening to spoil the day ...

A NEWSPAPER OFFICE, LANCASHIRE

When arriving at work in the morning the last thing you would think about is what has been happening there during the night while the office was closed. But if you were to work in one newspaper office in Lancashire it might well occasionally cross your mind. This particular office is said to have once been a doctor's surgery so it comes as no surprise that the building jumps with activity in a paranormal sense.

Many unexplainable spooky occurrences are said to have taken place in the offices that have concerned and intrigued both workers and ghost hunters alike. One such event happened to a man who was visiting the office after dark. After sitting down to have a cup of coffee the man got up and then realised that a small area of the cord trousers he was wearing looked as though it had been burnt and was now stuck to his leg. The man was not a smoker so was not carrying a lighter or indeed any matches in his pocket that might have caused the trousers to burn. It was as if the trousers had been melted like nylon for no apparent reason. If some of the coffee he had been drinking had spilt this would certainly not have caused the trousers to melt in this way, so it was a rather startling thing to happen.

Loud unexplained bangs have been heard frequently in the office and doors have been known to open and close unaided. People have sensed the presence of many invisible beings floating around the offices and described the unnerving feeling of being watched. At times some have even thought that these unseen beings were rushing past them at a great speed. Black shadows have been witnessed acting in this way as if they are running around the premises. Is it these mysterious manifestations that are causing the loud bangs and strange noises that resonate in this space?

Another scary event happened when a torch lying on a table spookily turned itself on when no-one was holding it or even anywhere near it. The apparition of a man dressed in clothing from the 1930s or 1940s has also been sighted. It is said he looked like he was walking the premises in a supervisory capacity, making sure that everything was in order and checking that the people who were wandering the office at night were not touching things they weren't meant to touch.

With this bounty of paranormal activity in this place of work, it is clearly not just the stories in the newspaper that are of interest.

A WAREHOUSE, WORKSOP, NOTTINGHAMSHIRE

There is an office complex and warehouse near Worksop that people fear to be alone in at night. Previously used as an army storage depot during the Second World War, it is said to be filled with frightening paranormal activity and the spirit of a soldier who tragically took his own life there. It is believed that he hung himself in the warehouse, in a corner up on the gallery floor. The reason for his suicidal action is not known but since this time there are many tales of people feeling that there was a presence within the complex.

The sound of mysterious footsteps resonates around the warehouse and corridors and many have witnessed what they believe to be a shadowy figure moving around this space. Dramatic changes in temperature have also been felt. It may well be that the tragic soldier is often drawn back to the place of his death.

Creepy Castles

Standing firm against attack, it is the invisible beings within the castle walls that now challenge its defences ...

THE TURRET GATEWAY, LEICESTER

Today very little remains of the magnificent Leicester Castle that once stood in the East Midlands city of Leicester. One section, however, still stands – a 14th-century gateway known as the Turret Gateway that used to lead from the precincts of the castle to a part of the city called the Newarkes.

Many battles were fought in this area, and the castle and the entire settlement of Leicester were once surrounded by walls to protect the town from attack. In the Siege of Leicester, which took place in 1645, Charles I and Prince Rupert overpowered the defenders of the city, among whom was John Bunyan who later went on to write one of English literature's most important works, *The Pilgrim's Progress.*

Many local legends surround the Turret Gateway including some involving a woman called Black Annis. She is believed to have lived in a cave on a heath in what is now a Leicester suburb two miles from the gateway. It is said she loved children so much that she used to catch them and devour their vital organs, hanging up their little skeletons, held together by skin, on bushes. When the supply of local children dried up, she dug a tunnel to the Turret Gateway and continued her activities in the town. The ghost of Black Annis is said to haunt the gateway and it has been spotted behind a door close by. She is said to scare adults and children with her witch-like appearance, broken teeth and nails, hideous face and shrill screams. Even dogs have been known to act strangely around the gateway.

Apart from Black Annis there is also thought to be the ghost of a lady who should have become Queen of England. At the age of twelve, Mary de Bohun married Henry Bolingbroke who later became King Henry IV but Mary died in childbirth some years before Henry became king. She bore him seven children, including the future Henry V. Her apparition is said to have been seen walking around the gateway on a number of occasions intriguing witnesses rather than terrifying them.

ELVASTON CASTLE, DERBYSHIRE

Elvaston Castle in Derbyshire dates back to the early 1800s, although there was an earlier manor house on the site. The inside of the castle is said to hold a number of dead souls and there have been reports of a number of ghosts trapped within the castle's structure. One such spooky entity is that of a grey lady, who is said to have been seen wandering the halls of the castle on a number of occasions but who she is and her connection to the castle remain a mystery.

The kitchen of the castle is also said to house the manifestation of a maid, trapped in time, carrying out the duties she would have performed when she was alive. It is possible that she may have loved her work so much that she could not bare to leave it behind when she died or maybe she just has some unfinished business. Whatever the reason for her continued presence it is apparent that she will continue to grace the kitchen of the castle for some time yet.

GOODRICH CASTLE, HEREFORDSHIRE

Goodrich Castle, nestling in the Wye Valley in Herefordshire, is said to be home to a ghostly love story.

The castle was first built in 1101 on its present site overlooking the River Wye. It was originally known as Godric Castle, after Godric Mapplestone, the founder and first owner of the castle's original earth and timber structure. Since then it has passed through many different hands and has been inhabited by many different families.

The ghostly love story linked to the castle has ensured the building is known widely as a place where hauntings take place. The love story belongs to Alice Birch, the niece of a Parliamentarian colonel, and Charles Clifford, a loyal Royalist. In 1645 on a stormy night, Alice and Charles were hiding at Goodrich Castle when a legion of Parliamentarians led by her uncle besieged the castle. Alice and Charles managed to flee on horseback but tragically both were drowned in the River Wye. It is said that on occasion their shrieks of terror and sorrowful screams can still be heard down by the river. Ghosts of the pair have spookily also been spotted wandering around the castle, along its walls and at the foot of its ruins. It is believed that every year Alice and Charles return on the anniversary of their death.

DONNINGTON CASTLE, NEWBURY, BERKSHIRE

Donnington Castle was built in 1386 on a hill in the small village of Donnington overlooking the town of Newbury in Berkshire. Now in ruins apart from the gatehouse, the castle has a long history of warfare and military occupation and many of the ghosts that are believed to wander the grounds are linked to these times. People believe they have witnessed the apparitions of guards in battle, defending the castle from invasion.

Some have also seen soldiers wandering around the castle's grounds dressed in clothes from the time of the Roman occupation of England, and other people are also said to have seen Royalist soldiers in the area.

Next to the castle gatehouse an apparition of a green lady has been seen asking visitors why the gates are closed before vanishing into thin air.

One night some people camping in the area believe they saw the ghostly form of an elderly Royalist soldier holding a young woman in a headlock amd pulling her hair. Alarmed by what was going on, one of the campers shouted at this vision, telling the soldier to leave the girl alone. The phantom soldier is then said to have growled back. The group then walked towards the apparitions and the soldier let out another much louder growl before disappearing along with the girl.

Could this have been the end of the poor unfortunate girl's life? Whoever the soldier was, he was surely an evil man and one to be feared.

Another ghost witnessed at the castle is that of a mystical white dog who has been seen running down the hill from the castle before vanishing.

With so many time periods reflected in the paranormal activity witnessed at the castle it is clear that a plethora of ghosts reside in the grounds. Anyone who dares to enter the grounds of the building after dark does so knowing they may well experience the fright of their lives at Donnington Castle.

DUNSTANBURGH CASTLE, NORTHUMBERLAND

Dunstanburgh Castle in Northumberland is thought by many to be a hotbed of paranormal activity. The castle ruins sit overlooking the North Sea, just as they have done for many hundreds of years.

Many ghosts are said to wander the site, with strange cold spots and an oppressive atmosphere felt by many within the castle walls. Also the feeling of being watched is a commonly reported experience, as is the frightening notion of being followed by an unknown invisible entity.

The most famous ghost of Dunstanburgh Castle is possibly that of Thomas, Earl of Lancaster, who built the castle. He was executed for treason in 1322 by King Edward II and it is believed his ghost still walks his former home.

Paranormal investigators have also noted seeing luminous figures outside the castle walls. Are these the spirits of former guards, still trying to defend the castle from attack, or are they simply apparitions of former dwellers of the castle, wandering aimlessly around in the vicinity of the castle?

CHILLINGHAM CASTLE, NORTHUMBERLAND

Chillingham Castle in Northumberland has the unenviable title of being one of the most haunted castles in England. Over eight hundred years old, the castle was built as part of the first line of English defence by Edward I against the invading Scots back in the days of William Wallace and Robert the Bruce. The castle has a very colourful and tumultuous history filled with killings, torture, death and deception.

Within the building itself there are certain areas with more paranormal activity than others. One of the more active areas is the dungeon, where prisoners were treated appallingly. If it was their fate to end their days within the dungeon, they would have been thrown down into the oubliette below, after having their arms and legs broken. An oubliette could only be accessed by a hatch in the ceiling and once in there many would die a truly excruciating death from starvation. Some would even resort to cannibalism by eating the flesh of fellow prisoners and sometimes even there own flesh to try and prolong their life. It is said that some visitors to the castle on looking down into the oubliette see the haunting remains of a young girl staring straight back up at them. No wonder the dungeon is said to have an oppressive and extremely depressing atmosphere with many people experiencing a variety of emotions in its depths.

The torture chamber within Chillingham Castle would also have been an ungodly and terrifying place where unimaginable pain was inflicted on people.

There is said to be an evil ghost within the chamber who could perhaps be the ghost of one of the torturers, still revelling in the pain of his victims. It is thought the malevolent spirit could be that of the most infamous and notorious torturer to work at the castle, a man by the name of John Sage. He hated the Scots and would revel in inflicting pain on the Scottish people captured and brought to the castle. Men, women and children who fell into his hands experienced terrible deaths.

One of the torture implements that would have been used at the time was a cage that was strapped to a prisoner's stomach with a starving rat inside. With no other way out, the rat would eat its way through the flesh of the prisoner's stomach causing agonising pain.

Another of the torture tools often used was a barrel that was filled with spikes. A prisoner would be shoved inside the barrel and then rolled around in it. The spikes would have ripped at the prisoner's body, causing unimaginable pain with every bump or turn of the barrel.

The most famous ghost of the castle is said to be that of the Blue Boy. His body was found in 1920, encased behind a wall in a room known as the 'pink room'. It is said that he was put in there alive along with important documents that were intended for the Spanish Armada. The poor boy would have tried everything to escape from within the wall before he lost his life; and the ghostly sound of scratching is said to be heard from this space, bringing to mind the boy's final hours as he tried in vain to get out of his prison. His cries of agony and fear at his impending death are also reputed to resonate from this area. People also claim to have seen strange flashes of blue light and a blue halo shape has been said to appear and move towards any people sleeping in the pink room.

Another soul not at rest whose presence is said to grace Chillingham Castle, is the ghost of Lady Berkeley. She was once married to Lord Grey, one of the former owners of the castle. Lord Grey is believed to have run off one night with Lady Henrietta, his wife's sister, leaving his wife and baby alone in the castle. It is thought that Lady Berkeley's ghost is still searching the castle for her husband and the sound of her dress swishing and rustling along the corridors of the castle has been heard. A sudden chill in the air accompanies this occurrence, ensuring that this ghostly event does not go unnoticed by whoever is near.

Chillingham Castle is undoubtedly a very scary place to visit after dark or during the day, and it is easy to see why it is known as one of the most haunted locations in all of England.

Edlingham Castle, Northumbria

The dilapidated ruins of Edlingham Castle are not widely renowned for ghosts stories, but there are few accounts of witnesses seeing first-hand paranormal happenings around the sparse crumbling stone structure. Spooky noises have been heard to resonate from the area and some people claim to have seen unexplainable lights darting around.

In the 1100s, a man by the name of John de Edlingham built a two-storey house on the spot where the ruins stand today. Later on in the 13th century Sir William de Felton expanded the structure and over the years the building was further improved, so by the 15th century the house was known as a castle. However, once the castle was no longer needed for defence it was eventually used as a farm building and animals were even kept in its lower floors. The castle was subsequently abandoned around 1650 and left to decay into further ruin. It is thought that around six foot of windswept soil now covers a great deal of what remains of Edlingham Castle.

The known paranormal activity that is said to have been experienced around the ancient ruins has made its self known in a variety of different ways, some scarier than others: the area where the old castle once stood has been described as having an oppressive and powerful atmosphere, with people sensing that they are being watched and even followed around the grounds by an invisible being; baffling lights have been spotted near the castle and in the adjacent fields around it, when no living being was present and no other creature could have made them; dark shadows resembling the figures of people have been witnessed skulking about, one even being mistaken for a real person – the black figure was seen sitting on a wall within the ruins before it vanished; unfathomable images have also been captured on film, with one, a gloved finger, seen from close up; and there have been reported incidents of people having their clothes tugged at in broad daylight by an unseen source.

It is said that over three hundred years ago a famous local witch named Margaret Stothard was put on trial on the site of the castle and some believe that her spirit could still be roaming the ruins.

A visitor to the castle, who was believed to be psychic, said that the playful spirit of a young girl also haunts the old castle. She is thought to tug people's clothes but for attention rather than to frighten them.

A rather more chilling entity is thought to be housed within the ruins – a ghost that wants to scare people away by making its presence felt. This particular ghoul is said to make loud noises and throw things around the ruins. Is this the perpetrator of the paranormal sounds which have resonated from within the tower of the old castle? Strange shuffling sounds have been heard coming from the tower followed by loud crashing noises coming down the stairs, as if a brick was being thrown, bouncing off the walls as it fell.

Another paranormal happening that took the form of very loud, heavy breathing is noted as coming from a spot in a nearby field and one of the people unfortunate enough to hear it was scared out of their wits. They described the noise as sounding like a dragon. Shrill screaming was also said to come from the same spot but on further inspection there was no living being in the vicinity, let alone a dragon.

Could it be the same angry spirit who is the source of all these scary noises, ensuring that anyone who visits

Edlingham Castle and the surrounding area feels very unwelcome indeed?

CASTLE KEEP, NEWCASTLE UPON TYNE

The Castle Keep of Newcastle upon Tyne is one of the north-east city's oldest buildings, dating back to the Norman period. The Castle Keep was built between 1168 and 1178 by Henry II on the site of an earlier castle built by Robert Curthose, son of William the Conqueror, in 1080. An Anglo-Saxon cemetery and the Roman fort of Pons Aelius have also existed on the same site.

The Castle Keep was the foundation for the thriving city that continues to expand today. It appears to be quite a small structure from the outside but step inside and the building opens up and feels much larger. With a building as old as the Castle Keep and the site on which it stands dating back almost 2,000 years, people will have lived in this space for a very long time and many occurrences both joyous and terrifying will have taken place over the years. There are sure to be many spirits who walk its dark, cold, eerie corridors and the keep is said to have a strange indescribable atmosphere, further heightening the prevalence of paranormal goings-on.

The garrison room within the building is said to

house the spirit of a poppy girl who met a truly tragic and terrifying end. She is said to have been locked in the garrison room with over thirty imprisoned soldiers, by whom she was raped and then beaten to death. Her petrified screams are said to resonate from this area to this day.

Another ghost said to haunt the keep by wandering its corridors is that of a strange cloaked figure wearing a top hat. Could it be that this man once lived within the castle?

People claim to have seen an endless number of sinister shadows on the walls and in the corners of rooms within the building, particularly in the upstairs gallery, ensuring that the Castle Keep is certainly not a place one would choose to wander in alone.

SCARBOROUGH CASTLE, YORKSHIRE

The ruins of the 12th-century Scarborough Castle nestle on a headland between the north and south bays of the town. Eight hundred years have taken their toll and only a small amount of the original structure can be seen today, nevertheless the castle still sits watchfully surveying the North Sea.

Over the centuries and right up until the end of the Second World War, the present Scarborough Castle has had many reincarnations. Originally built as a royal fortress by Edward II, it was heavily damaged during the English Civil War and subsequently part of the structure became a prison. The castle remained a prison for a long period before eventually it became, in its fnal guise, a secret listening post during the Second World War.

Folklore suggests that there is a lot of paranormal activity in the castle grounds and this has manifested in the form of a sinister troublesome ghost from the 14th century. Most of the spooky occurrences that have taken place around this area have been on the outer walls of the castle. It is said that the headless spirit of a favoured subject of King Edward II, a man by the name of Piers Gaveston, haunts the dilapidated ruins. Reputedly he attempts to lure people over the edge of the cliffs to their deaths. Many people have felt as though they were being pushed frighteningly towards the edge of the cliffs and some even claim to have heard the cackling laugh of a man whilst this was happening. With such a dastardly spirit resident in the grounds of the castle, you are sure to get a scare when venturing around the once grand and imposing Scarborough Castle at night.

WHORLTON CASTLE, YORKSHIRE

The dilapidated ruins of a once grand castle with a fascinating history stand amidst the north Yorkshire Moors. The land on which Whorlton Castle forlornly stands today has been occupied for many hundreds of years and it is believed that a wooden fort stood proudly on this spot as far back as the 12th century. Over the centuries the castle has been owned by three different families, the De Meynells, the Darcys and the Strangways and it has played host to noblemen and even royalty. Edward II is believed to have hunted in the deer parks at Whorlton, enjoying the thrill of the chase in its grounds. Much later, during the English Civil War, it is believed that Royalists held the castle as it was bombarded by Cromwell's Parliamentarians.

With such an interesting history it comes as no surprise that the plethora of paranormal activity that has been experienced at the old castle would send a shudder down any person's spine. Some people walking around the ruins have had the unnerving sensation of being touched by someone or something they cannot see. One visitor is known to have had their head touched and another their ear. Both people had instantly felt that another living person was touching them, only to turn around and find that there was no-one there.

Unsuspecting visitors have also experienced the feeling of being watched while many have had the notion that someone was walking past them. Some have told of how they felt as if a group of people were walking towards them and encircling them. People have also described how their body temperature has risen dramatically in some areas of the ruined building, as if they were burning up with a sudden fever.

Dark figures have been spotted moving around; it is said to be hard to ascertain the gender of the figures that appear in shadowy forms lurking around Whorlton Castle. Reputedly, the vision of a phantom dog was spotted – was it looking for its old master in its former home?

The presence of a lady named Elizabeth Meynell has been felt in the ruins. Elizabeth was married to one of the castle's former owners, a man named Robert Darcy. Her apparition is said to have appeared dressed in grey clothing but disappeared very quickly shortly after. People are curious as to why she continues to haunt the ruins all these centuries after her death. Did she love the place so much that she does not want to leave or did her life experience a traumatic ending which is forcing her soul to stay within the castle walls?

Some visitors claim to have heard paranormal sound phenomena and on one occasion this took the form of a mysterious loud sigh that had no visible source.

Whorlton Castle is certainly a place that should be entered with some trepidation – you may come face to face with something more frightening than the ruins of an old castle.

PENGERSICK CASTLE, PRAA SANDS, CORNWALL

The Pengersick Castle that stands today in the village of Praa Sands in Cornwall is a fortified Tudor dwelling although the site on which it sits has been lived on since the Bronze Age.

In the Middle Ages a family settled properly on the site and took the name of Pengersick as their own. A man by the name of Henry Pengersick later married Engrina Godolphin, the daughter of a nearby estate owner. The outline of the original manor house that they lived in, the chapel, the gardens and a nearby village settlement have all been discovered by archaeologists.

Around the year 1500 John Milliton built the castle that we see today. However, it was his son, also called John, who was part of one of the most notable periods in the castle's history when the King of Portugal's treasure ship, the *St. Anthony*, was wrecked off the coast near to Pengersick Castle. On board were thousands of pounds worth of treasures but most of it vanished mysteriously from the ship's wreck. Manorial rights meant that local landowners had the right to assume ownership of the ship's haul and they appeared to take full advantage of this, John Milliton included.

The castle is said to house paranormal activity in a variety of forms and on a very grand scale. It is noted as being a rather atmospheric building and many strange and spooky occurrences have been reported by people who have visited there over the years.

Some have said that they have felt like they were being watched by unknown entities, with unseen eyes following their every move not only in the grounds of the castle but also in the building itself.

The grounds of the castle are also thought to teem with haunting goings-on. A young female figure in ghostly form has been spotted walking into the wall on the east side of the castle before disappearing. In the woods within the grounds visitors have heard stones being thrown around them but not from a human hand as there was no-one else there. The haunting sound of galloping horses' hooves have also been heard, stopping people in their tracks with amazement.

Step inside the castle and a plethora of paranormal activity is waiting to be witnessed. Unexplainable noises resonating from no known living source are heard often throughout the castle and doors have been known to open and close on their own. General feelings of nausea and dizziness have been felt by perfectly healthy people in different areas of the castle, but in particular in the gunnery room. Dark looming shadows have also been witnessed creeping around the walls of the building, ready to frighten anyone who sees them. Lots of sudden flashes of light in the castle have been reported by individuals who have walked the building and grounds after dark.

It is said that over thirty separate ghosts have been identified at the castle but some appear to have more credence than others. These have been in the form of mysterious figures seen moving around the corridors and rooms, as well as some full apparitions. Whoever the spirits of Pengersick Castle are it appears they dwell in a place they once thought of as home.

PENDENNIS CASTLE, FALMOUTH, CORNWALL

Pendennis Castle sits on Pendennis Head in Cornwall, one mile south-east of Falmouth. It was built over 450 years ago under the instructions of Henry VIII and formed part of the defence created by Henry against the threat of invasion from Spain and other mainland European countries. Indeed right up to, and throughout, the Second World War the castle has protected England's south-west coast from her enemies.

The castle is thought to be the home of more than eight ghosts, including a Lieutenant Governor and a scullery girl and a former head cook who both worked at the castle. A busy kitchen maid is also believed to haunt the staircase of the castle after she reportedly fell to her death whilst carrying a tray of food. Her shrill screams as she fell have been heard by some around the staircase area.

Within the Tudor kitchen there is said to be a ghost who produces the sound of footsteps on the staircase, even though the stairs no longer lead anywhere; and in the keep of Pendennis Castle the ghost of a woman has been heard humming near the stairs – an occurrence that sends a shiver of fear through anyone unfortunate enough to hear her haunting song.

One witness to an apparition has spoken about how he saw somebody standing at the bottom of the stairs in the keep. The ghostly figure is then said to have spoken to the man and said, 'I'm here on the wall.'

Automatically the man glanced in the direction of the fireplace where he saw pictures of people on the wall. He was drawn instinctively to one picture in particular and believes it is because the person in it was the very same one whose spirit was now communicating with him.

In the half-moon battery of the castle whistling has been heard that alters in both pitch and noise level, while furniture is known to creak in areas around the castle for some unfathomable reason.

With so much paranormal activity occurring in Pendennis Castle it is undoubtedly somewhere you should enter with some trepidation after dark.

Petrifying Places of Worship

They come to worship, they come to pray but many of the spirits who appear simply refuse to go away ...

St. Mary's Church, Avenbury, Herefordshire

In the small village of Avenbury, which sits on the banks of the River Froome, there is a hidden ruined church. The ruins of St. Mary's Church, overgrown with brambles and trees, sit solemnly in the countryside in a secluded and somewhat secret spot.

Before it fell into decay and ruin, St. Mary's Church was a fine piece of architecture with a nave, chancel, porch and a square tower that housed three bells within it. Today, however, relatively little remains of the church that was first built around 870 AD and then rebuilt in Norman times. Mother Nature and history have taken their toll. Only a small section still stands, along with the fallen and broken gravestones of long-dead people that lie around it.

On first inspection you would presume that the church had stood empty and unused for many centuries, but in fact it has been closed for less than a hundred years. For, after years of St. Mary's falling into disrepair and many people taking on its renovation over the centuries, the church closed for the final time in 1931 and has stood forlornly crumbling ever since.

With such a long history it is no surprise that the ruins of the church are said to hold a plethora of paranormal activity. In 1919 the sound of the organ being played was heard from outside the church despite the fact that no-one was in the building and the church was locked up at the time. This haunting organ music has been heard on a number of occasions both before and after the church closed its doors for the final time.

It is also believed that the churchyard at St. Mary's was the victim of grave robbers who used the churchyard and its occupants to carry out black magic rituals.

A terrifying ghostly event was witnessed by a church warden one day as he walked around the grounds of the building he tended. The man is said to have seen a funeral taking place, but when he looked a little closer he noticed that the mourners at the graveside were not living beings but a group of phantom monks. Another unusual funeral was described by a lady who was walking around the church and thought she saw a burial taking place. However, on closer inspection she noticed that none of the mourners had heads!

A man by the name of Nicholas Vaughn is said to haunt the grounds in which St. Mary's Church once stood. Following his death by execution, the hauntings around the churchyard were apparently so frequent that Vaughn's body was dug up and reburied in a silver box that was submerged by a flowing brook next to the church. A large stone was then placed over the spot and when the brook becomes shallow enough the stone can be seen sticking out of the water. In line with the superstitions of the time, people believed that if the box that held Nicholas Vaughn's body was covered by flowing water, his ghost would not be able to rise up and haunt the area.

There is, however, another tale linked to the stone. A brother and sister who lived in the area from the early 1900s claimed that the body of a woman who was thought to be a witch lay beneath it. It is said that the villagers would not allow her to be buried in the graveyard but agreed that she could be buried near to the church.

Whoever it is that lies beneath the stone in the brook, they were placed there because the villagers believed they should not lie at rest in the consecrated ground of St. Mary's Church and whatever their crime it must surely have weighed heavy with the local people.

DERBY CATHEDRAL, DERBY

Derby Cathedral is situated in the very heart of the city of Derby. The original church was founded by King Edmund I in about 943 but the cathedral as it now stands dates from the 1400s. Much of the cathedral was rebuilt in 1725, and although it is the smallest Anglican cathedral in England it still has its own air of grandeur and has been a venue for innumerable celebrations and events for over five hundred years.

Derby Cathedral is said to be home to a number of spirits, both inside its walls and in its grounds. A white lady is reported to have been seen standing on the steps to the cathedral. She is said to appear quickly and disappear again just as quickly. It is not known who this lady is and why she stands alone on the steps and out in the cold, but whatever her reasons it is apparent that Derby Cathedral is her home for now and possibly for many years to come.

It is also said that the tragic figure of a crying woman carrying a young child has been seen around the cathedral. This distressing vision has been witnessed on a number of occasions by many different people. Other apparitions that people claim to have witnessed include that of a man wearing old-fashioned clothes walking in the area.

GRACEDIEU PRIORY RUINS, LEICESTERSHIRE

Dating from the 1200s, Gracedieu Priory has a long history. Over many years, it was home to nuns of the Augustinian Order. However, life at the priory came to an abrupt end when it was dissolved in 1538. The ruins stand in the floor of a valley bounded by a small brook on the edge of Charnwood Forest on the A512 road from Loughborough to Ashby de la Zouch in Leicestershire.

It is the A512 itself which is said to have experienced a multitude of paranormal happenings and many people are said to have witnessed ghostly figures on or around this route.

The most famous ghost story connected to the ruins was witnessed by an entire bus load of people back in the 1950s. On seeing someone waiting at the bus stop opposite the ruins, the driver of the bus is said to have pulled over to pick up the woman, who was dressed all in white. On opening the door of the bus the driver found that she had vanished. Concerned he got out of his bus and had a look around but could not see anyone. The manifestation of the woman was so lifelike that all the bus passengers were equally puzzled for they had all witnessed the lady in white. Could she be a former nun still walking near the grounds of the priory she once lived in? It would appear so.

Accounts of people seeing the ghosts of nuns in white habits around this area are plentiful. Sometimes a group of the apparitions walking together has been seen so undoubtedly there is more than one dead soul gracing the area. Many of these sightings have been seen along the same stretch of road where the bus encountered the white lady back in the 1950s.

You may be wondering why it is that in these apparent sightings the nuns of Gracedieu Priory wear white habits and not black. This is not because the colour of their clothes has changed with death but because it is said that all those hundreds of years ago when the Sisters of Gracedieu Priory were alive they chose to wear white rather than black habits. The fact that ghostly nuns are still to be seen walking near the grounds of their former home would suggest that they want to stay close to the place where they once worshipped.

GODSTOW ABBEY, OXFORDSHIRE

Godstow Abbey in Oxfordshire was built during the 1130s for nuns of the Benedictine Order. During its early life the abbey was extended thanks to generous donations by King Henry II, who held the place dear to his heart. It is recounted in history that his mistress Rosamund was buried there and that this is the reason why he endowed the abbey. After nearly four hundred years the abbey was closed due to Henry VIII's Second Act of Dissolution in which hundreds of Catholic monasteries and religious houses were destroyed.

After a long period of time Godstow Abbey was converted into Godstow House by a man named George Owen, but during the English Civil War the house was badly damaged, and after this it fell into disrepair. With such a considerable life span and interesting history Godstow Abbey has always intrigued paranormal enthusiasts and ghost hunters, eager to find out what happens after dark in the old nunnery. It would be safe to assume that this place is filled with the souls of the long-departed nuns still carrying out their practical and spiritual duties.

People who have dared to walk in the grounds after dark have reputedly heard unusual sounds and odd noises throughout the ruins, but it is hard to tell whether these come from the surrounding wildlife or indeed from paranormal activity. Whatever their source, they are sure to create questions in even the most sceptical of minds.

The Church of St. Mary de Castro, Leicester

In the city of Leicester's old town there are five medieval churches. The Church of St. Mary de Castro is one of them and it dates back as far as the early 12th century and possibly even before. The church is thought by some to be the last resting place of Mary de Bohun (see page 104). It is the apparent ghostly goings-on in the church's graveyard that have interested visitors and locals alike. For it is believed that the area around St. Mary de Castro is rife with paranormal activity.

One incident occurred when a local tour guide was showing a party around the churchyard. After he had finished telling them some ghostly tales from the area, something extremely spooky occurred. A young lady walking beside him, who he had assumed was part of his group, told him that her name was Elizabeth Simons. Just as she said this he glanced down at a gravestone and to his amazement it bore the same name. In an instant the lady disappeared into the crowd never to be seen again. The guide believes that the young woman he spoke to could well have been the ghost of the woman in the grave!

Later when he was recounting this experience to another of his tour groups, the spirit of Elizabeth Simons seemed to manifest again but this time in a different form – people in the group told of how they saw a grey cloudy mist circling around the back of the guide's head as he was telling them about her.

Why the ghostly vision of Elizabeth appeared is not known. It could be that she was simply interested in the people chattering around her grave and wanted them to know that she was still there, wandering as a spirit in the churchyard of the old Church of St. Mary de Castro.

LYDIATE ABBEY, MERSEYSIDE

In the village of Lydiate in Merseyside there stands a ruined abbey with a macabre and sinister history. Known locally as St. Catherine's Chapel, the abbey was built as a private chapel for the family of Lawrence Ireland who lived nearby in Lydiate Hall. Its use as a private chapel probably ceased around 1550 as a result of Henry VIII's dissolution of the monasteries.

Some visitors to the forlorn, crumbling remains of this ancient abbey experience feelings of deep revulsion, possibly because the abbey has reputedly been exposed to ungodly amd disturbing acts over the centuries. It is said, for example, that it has borne witness to human sacrifices, including that of babies and children.

Although merely a shell with no roof, Lydiate Abbey is said to house paranormal activity on a sinister scale. Crying and screaming that sound as if they are coming from both adults and children and sometimes even from babies have been know to ring out from this place. Could these sounds possibly be the ghostly wails of the terrified victims of human sacrifice?

EGGLESTONE ABBEY, COUNTY DURHAM

Egglestone Abbey in County Durham was once a magnificent building but over the years time has taken its toll on the late 12th-century building. Not much of the original structure stands today but the grounds and the ruins that still remain are reputedly home to numerous spirits.

It is believed that one such soul is that of a monk who still visits in spirit form. He is said to have conducted secret trysts with a local girl down by the banks of the River Tees and the two fell in love. However, racked with guilt over the sin he was committing, the monk took one final trip down to the banks of the river to meet his lover. He is thought to have become enraged at the sight of her and strangled her to death before throwing her body into the river. It is said that bloodcurdling screams can still be heard down by the river in the dead of night. The last hopeless cries perhaps of the young woman – looking into the eyes of the man she loved as he killed her – echoing hauntingly from beyond the grave?

The tragic tale does not end there, for after committing this evil act the monk went back to the abbey, tormented by his deeds and overcome with guilt. And soon after he is thought to have thrown himself into the river's consuming waters, thus ending his own life and the tragic story of his forbidden love. On numerous occasions people have seen the apparition of a monk walking down from the abbey to the banks of the River Tees and some have even seen what looked like the figure of a lady with him.

St. Clether Holy Chapel and Well, Cornwall

In the small picturesque village of St. Clether in Cornwall there is said to be one of the oldest holy wells in the county. Originally built in the 5th century, the well and the chapel are constructed in such a way that the spring water which collects in the upper wellhouse runs through the chapel and underneath the granite altar, re-emerging in the lower well before continuing on to join the River Inny. Time after time over the centuries the chapel and well have fallen into ruin only to be restored again. Restoration was carried out in the 15th century, then in the 19th century when the Reverend Sabine Baring-Gould rebuilt the chapel between 1895–1900, and more recently in the 21st century, when in 2009 the chapel was restored to the beautiful structure that stands today.

There are a number of paranormal stories attached to the St. Clether Holy Chapel and Well that have been recounted by many over the years. One of the most famous tells of a mysterious figure who has been spotted on a number of occasions inside the chapel. The apparition is thought to be that of Reverend Baring-Gould because he loved the building so much.

The sound of horses' hooves has also been heard resonating from around the chapel, when no horses have been anywhere near the area. Another paranormal occurrence that took place inside the chapel has been captured on camera and took the form of a grey mist that appeared inside the building during a church service. The mist appears to have two shapes coming out of it that look like wings. Could this be an angelic being, floating around the old building? Audio recordings taken within the chapel when no-one was there have spookily picked up loud knocks and bangs.

St. Clether Holy Chapel and Well appears to be quaint little place but if you are left alone there as the sun sets the old building becomes an altogether different space.

WHITBY ABBEY, NORTH YORKSHIRE

The town of Whitby in Yorkshire is famous for its fish and chips and seaside location. Whitby is believed to have been founded in 657 AD by the Anglo-Saxon King of Northumbria, Oswy, and was named Streoneshalh. Long before this time it is thought that a Roman settlement may have been built there also.

Standing high above Whitby harbour there sits the imposing shell of Whitby Abbey, a former Benedictine monastery. In 867 AD the original structure fell to a Viking attack and was subsequently abandoned. Later in its history, in 1078, it is believed that a man named William de Percy ordered the abbey to be re-founded. The second monastery, which still stands on the same spot today, was in use until 1540. At this point Henry VIII saw fit to order his troops to plunder the abbey for its treasures and ultimately destroy the building and its monastery during the dissolution of the monasteries. The abbey slowly succumbed to nature and much of its stone was taken and used elsewhere in the area. Sailors, however, would still look for the ruins of the abbey to navigate themselves safely to Whitby Port.

The ghost of Constance De Beverly, a young nun who broke her vows by falling in love with a knight, is said to wander the area to this day. It is believed that Constance and her lover used to meet secretly in the grounds of a nearby cemetery but one terrible evening they were discovered. Legend has it that Constance was taken to the abbey and imprisoned in a tower. It is said that the door to the tower was then bricked up leaving her inside. Unable to escape and with no food and water, she starved to death.

The ghosts of Constance and her knight are said to have been witnessed walking around the abbey ruins and meeting up in the graveyard. Have they succeeded in being together in death after failing to do so when they were alive?

Haunted Hotels

A place to rest a weary head, but when closing your eyes and lying in bed, be sure to watch out for the presence of the dead ...

Bestwood Lodge, Arnold, Nottinghamshire

Bestwood Lodge sits in the village of Arnold in Nottinghamshire some three miles from Nottingham city centre. Arnold was once part of the royal hunting forest of Sherwood as was the royal forest of Bestwood. Bestwood Forest is mentioned frequently over many reigns and the first hunting lodge was built there around 1363. The hotel building as it now stands was built in 1863 as a Victorian hunting lodge and is set in some 700 acres of parkland.

During its lifetime the hotel has taken on a variety of

guises. It was the headquarters for the British Army's Northern Command during the Second World War and after the evacuation of Dunkirk, Bestwood Lodge provided a temporary respite for some of the 311,000 British and French soldiers traumatised after facing an uncertain future on a French beach.

Bestwood Lodge is thought to hold the spirits of some long-dead folk, including the spirit of a woman who manifests herself as a grey lady.

Frightening noises are said to haunt the building and some claim to have heard the cries and groaning of an injured soldier in different parts of the hotel. No-one knows who this person was and why his spirit still resides in the building. It is possible that these stomach-churning sounds come from a soldier killed in action, whose spirit returns to the barracks which were once his home, or perhaps he was fatally injured in the barracks themselves and now his soul haunts his final resting place.

One thing is certain – any hotel guest hearing these scary sounds is unlikely to rest easy in their bed.

The Crown and Thistle Hotel, Abingdon, Oxfordshire

The market town of Abingdon sits on the banks of the River Thames in Oxfordshire and has long prospered from its riverside location. Move away from the river banks and venture into the centre of the town and you will find the Crown and Thistle Hotel. A 17th-century coaching inn, the hotel has had people stopping for refreshments and overnight rest for almost four hundred years. Over this period of time the former coaching inn will have witnessed many differing types of events and will undoubtedly have borne witness to the darker side of human nature.

The whitewashed Crown and Thistle is said to house the ghost of a phantom horseman, whose horse's hooves have been heard clip-clopping around the courtyard of the hotel. It has been said that the vision of a carriage with four horses has also been seen to enter the hotel courtyard and cross to where the stables once stood. Rather than frightening the people who witness this event, it would surely be a sight to behold. This occurrence would after all have undoubtedly been a frequent happening in the days before cars and it does not seem unusual that such apparitions are witnessed in this place.

THE FEATHERS, LUDLOW, SHROPSHIRE

The medieval market town of Ludlow sits in the Welsh Marches, surrounded by picturesque hills and countryside and with the River Teme's waters flowing through it. The town attracts visitors from all over the world and coachloads of American tourists are a regular sight in the town. All are drawn to Ludlow by its history, quaintness and picturesque layout. The old market square is surrounded by beautiful buildings and even has its very own medieval castle, built as a stronghold against invasion by the Welsh. Many important historical figures have visited Ludlow Castle through the centuries, including Mary Tudor – Henry VIII's firstborn daughter lived at the castle for a number of years after she was sent there by her father during his marriage to Anne Boleyn.

However, step away from the market square and take a wander through the side alleys and streets and you will come across a famous hotel which many notable dignitaries and famous folk have frequented. The impressive Feathers Hotel, whose name springs from the motifs of ostrich feathers forming part of its black and white timber facade, has stood a short walk away from Ludlow's town centre for over four hundred years.

The Feathers was built in 1619 by a man named Rees Jones who was an attorney in the town, and it first saw life as a coaching inn around 1670. With food and flowing ale on offer, weary travellers would drop in to recuperate before continuing on their long journeys. Over the centuries, the Feathers has seen thousands of visitors come through its doors. It was a regular meeting place for people with entertainment often laid on for its customers. The cruel sport of cockfighting is known to have taken place there, with people placing bets as they jeered and hollered at two cockerels ripping feathers and flesh from each other.

An old bullring stood just along the road and people

used to flock there to indulge in the blood sport of bull baiting, in which dogs were set upon a bull while men gambled on the outcome of the fight. With easy access to such macabre but popular entertainment, the Feathers would have been a very busy place.

The inn was also a centre for political matters in the town with meetings held there and candidates for parliamentary elections preaching their policies from the balcony of the building.

It is not only the living who enjoy the comforts of the Feathers Hotel today. Some long-dead people are said to still reside within the walls of the Jacobean building and paranormal activity is plentiful with people witnessing apparitions and feeling the presence of unseen souls around them. The figure of a Victorian man and his dog have been seen by many and are said to walk through the walls of one room and straight into another; a mysterious entity is believed to wander the hotel opening doors; people have heard echoing footsteps around the hotel that do not appear to come from any living being; and the rather strange sound of hands clapping together has also been heard coming from an unseen source.

There is also believed to be the spirit of a lady who has taken a dislike to women staying at the hotel. During one incident a man and a woman were fast asleep in the hotel when the woman's hair was pulled so violently that she was dragged out of her bed and onto the floor. The man experienced quite the opposite when he felt something lovingly stroke his face – frightening occurrences for them both. The lady is then believed to have returned to bed but awoke to find her nightclothes were drenched with water.

With such a rich history, it is quite possible that many more souls may roam the Feathers Hotel, manifesting themselves in a multitude of different ways.

PENGETHLEY MANOR, NEAR ROSS-ON WYE, HEREFORDSHIRE

The picturesque Pengethley Manor near Ross-on-Wye in Herefordshire is said to be a hot spot of paranormal activity. Only four miles north of the historic market town of Ross-on-Wye, Pengethley Manor is a beautiful Georgian country manor set in 15 acres of ground and surrounded by National Trust parkland.

It is thought that a plethora of spirits reside within this 18th-century hotel. One particular ghost is reputed to be that of a young girl named Harriet, who tragically died during a fire which badly damaged Pengethley Manor in 1816. It is believed that the little girl became trapped within the property as the fire raged and was unable to escape the consuming flames. Harriet is thought to still wander the hotel and she could well be the perpetrator of some of the unexplainable paranormal occurrences.

The ghost of an old lady wearing a long black dress, is also said to reside in the hotel and she has been sighted on many occasions. She has been seen walking about in various different places in the hotel including the old cellar, the reception area and the library. No-one knows who this lady is and mystery surrounds the reason for her still inhabiting the hotel in spirit form.

According to some, another frequent ghostly happening is the sound of mysterious footsteps that can be heard throughout the hotel. Sending fear into both staff and visitors alike, there is no known source for the noise. Whoever these footsteps belong to, it would seem that they are frantically pacing up and down, still trapped inside the building in which they once lived and possibly died.

THE GREEN DRAGON, HEREFORD

In the cathedral city of Hereford there is an old hotel whose history is thought to date back to 1079 when it was a small local inn. It is said that when the construction of the nearby cathedral was taking place the workmen stayed at the inn and called it home for a time. Before being given its current name in 1706, the hotel was known as The White Lion. Many distinguished men are said to have stayed within the building over the centuries.

Two such men were the Earl of March and Owen Tudor. The Earl of March, who later became King Edward IV, is known to have stayed there after the

Battle of Mortimer's Cross in 1461, during the War of the Roses. He and his Yorkist followers fought and defeated the Lancastrians of Owen Tudor and his son Jasper during the battle. Jasper escaped but his father was captured and taken to Hereford to be executed and while awaiting execution he stayed in the old White Lion.

It is said Owen was a very handsome man with many female admirers and after his head was chopped off in Hereford's High Town, some women are believed to have washed his hair and placed his decapitated head on a cushion surrounded by candles.

The hotel would have welcomed many customers during the 18th century as it was an important coaching inn and a starting point for the long and tiring stagecoach journey to London.

During the Second World War many Hereford residents went down into the Green Dragon's cellar for safety during German air raids. In the cellar there is a secret tunnel, now partially blocked, that leads to Hereford Cathedral. In much earlier times the city's resident monks may have walked through this to get to their place of work and worship.

Today the hotel is said to house ghostly beings. Most of the paranormal activity has taken place on the third floor of the building: a strange presence has been felt along the corridors and many people sleeping there overnight claim to have felt very uncomfortable; and shadows have been witnessed slowly creeping around the floor when no living person is there to make them.

With a history dating back so far the ghosts that

haunt The Green Dragon may well be mingling with the dead of many different centuries.

The Queens Hotel, Bridlington, Yorkshire

In Bridlington's old town, the dead are said to dwell amongst the living. Many have borne witness to paranormal activity and people who have lived in this particular area of the Yorkshire seaside town have come to realise that ghosts wander the streets and reside within their homes.

Within the old town there once stood a large monastery and local legend has it that tunnels run underneath the streets down to the harbour and local monks once used them to transport food and drink into the town. Not much of the monastery remains: during his time as King of England, Henry VIII saw fit to destroy many of England's religious houses and today only the entrance, known as Bayle Gate, the Priory Church and a few archery mounts called Butts Close still stand.

The Queens Hotel on the High Street is located near to these ruins and this could be why a plethora of paranormal activity is said to have been witnessed here. The hotel was originally two separate buildings that were converted into one, merging the apparent spooky happenings of both the properties.

A lady who lived in the hotel with her family some

152

years ago has recounted the startling occurrences that she experienced there. She heard the haunting sound of something (she thought maybe it was boxes) being dragged along the floor in the room above her living room. But could this strange noise be a much more sinister sound resonating from a time long gone by? After hearing these eerie sounds, she went upstairs to investigate only to find nothing there except some old furniture. Mysterious footsteps have also been heard walking the floorboards in the dead of night before slowly fading away.

Because she had seen the mystifying apparition of a skull floating around her room on several occasions, the lady's sister was so terrified that she refused to sleep in her own bedroom. This particular room was often unnaturally freezing cold and the family dog was averse to entering it. Instead it would position itself at the door with its fur standing on end and bark angrily. It is believed that two people may have died within the building but with the age and locality of this hotel, many more will undoubtedly have met their maker in and around the Queens Hotel.

Arnos Manor Hotel, Arnos Vale, Bristol

The grand building now known as the Arnos Manor Hotel in Arnos Vale was built by a business man named William Reeve in 1760 as a family home. In

1851, after quite a few other owners, the house and the estate on which it sits were given to the Sisters of the Order of the Good Shepherd. The Grade-II listed structure closed as a convent during the Second World War, before becoming a private club and then finally the hotel that stands today.

The building is thought to house numerous spirits from different periods in its history, including ghost children who eerily walk the stairs of the hotel and the religious apparitions of long-dead monks and nuns.

One such ghost is thought to be the spirit of a nun named Sister Teresa, who is believed to have risen from the dead after a builder unearthed her mortal body in a stairwell in the house. Her ghostly grey image has been spotted gliding around the hotel's corridors and stairs.

Close to the spot where she was unearthed there is a wall on which the face of a beautiful lady with long, dark curly hair is said to appear. It is understood that she has an air of calmness and looks to be of strong character. It seems likely that this is a vision of Sister Teresa herself and it would appear that for some reason she continues to walk where she once lived. Why was she buried beneath the stairs within the old convent? Does she appear as a ghost because there is something unfinished concerning her death? These questions will remain forever unanswered but will continue to intrigue both ghost hunters and visitors to the Arnos Manor Hotel.

BORINGDON HALL, PLYMOUTH

On the outskirts of the naval town of Plymouth, the grand Boringdon Hall stands within its own grounds on the edge of the captivating countryside of Dartmoor. A Grade-I listed Elizabethan manor house, the building has played host to many famous figures in history including Elizabeth I, Sir Francis Drake and Sir Walter Raleigh. Boringdon Hall is mentioned in the Domesday Book – one of the earliest accounts of it as a permanent structure. The name 'Boringdon' derives from the Saxon 'Burth-Y-Don' meaning 'enchanted place on the hill'.

Some of the building that stands today and those that stood on the site before were all owned by the local priory of St. Peter until the dissolution of the monasteries under Henry VIII. Parliamentarians destroyed part of the hall during the Civil War and later it became a farmhouse before falling into disrepair.

Today the hall is a hotel that plays host to weddings and other celebrations, but it is the activities after dark that make Boringdon Hall a very interesting but scary place to visit. It is said that the old hall houses a plethora of spirits, all eager to frighten anyone living that dares to walk its corridors and rooms in darkness. Many male and female presences from different periods of history have reputedly been felt throughout the building including a ten-year-old girl from the Victorian era and man who was believed to have died in a fire back in the 1400s.

Whoever the many men and women who grace the building are, they make their presence felt in a variety of paranormal ways: there are said to be cold spots in some of the rooms that are quite simply hard to explain and light anomalies have been seen on night vision video cameras; strange shapes that move suddenly around rooms have also been spotted; a mysterious tapping sosund made by no living source has also been heard in the hall; and in the staircase area weird rattling noises have been heard that no-one can explain.

However, the most frightening thing of all has to be the sound of growling coming from outside one of the windows when there is no sign of anyone close by. Whoever or whatever is making this noise, they certainly seem to be perturbed by the presence of people inside Boringdon Hall.

The Iron Duke Hotel, Hove, East Sussex

The Iron Duke Hotel was built in 1823 as a coaching inn and was originally named the Kerrison Arms, but since then it has had a number of names and many different landlords. The hotel stands in the Brunswick Town area of Hove which is one of the most historically preserved Georgian planned communities in the south of England.

Across the road from the hotel there stands the Regency church of St. Andrews, which was built around the same time as the Iron Duke. It is the only church in Hove to have burial vaults under the church and there is said to be a secret underground tunnel that connects the church to the Iron Duke Hotel. It is believed that the main use for the tunnel in Victorian times was to allow distinguished members of society to slip into the inn for a drink after a church service unnoticed by the lower classes.

The Iron Duke hotel is said to be a hotbed of ghostly activity, as paranormal investigation teams have found out. Cold spots have been felt throughout the building and some people have stated that they felt someone putting a hand on their shoulder in the bar area. Could this hand belong to a long-departed drinker who still pops into the Iron Duke for a swift pint, as he would have done when alive?

In the toilets of the hotel there is said to be a strange presence and unexplainable strange noises have been heard coming from this area. The bedrooms of the hotel are also thought to be haunted and the spirit of a lady has been felt in one of them. Others have witnessed the figure of an elderly man in the hallway. Could these people be former guests of the hotel?

Down in the cellar of the old inn poltergeist activity has been witnessed on many occasions by staff, both old and new. The presence of a large intimidating man has been seen and felt on numerous occasions here. When a local paranormal investigation team ventured down to the creepy cellar, they heard many unexplainable noises including knocking sounds on the barrels of beer and scratches and bangs on the ceiling. With so many people passing through the building over time, it is easy to see why ghosts dwell at the Iron Duke Hotel.

THE CASTLE OF COMFORT HOTEL, NETHER STOWEY, SOMERSET

The Castle of Comfort Hotel sits on a quiet road near Bridgwater in Somerset. The Grade-II listed building dates back to the 16th century. A coaching inn during the 17th century and later a cider house, the building was turned into a private house and now stands as a country house hotel.

The hotel plays host to a plethora of paranormal goings-on: downstairs many taps and knockings and loud heavy footsteps have been heard coming from upstairs, where ghosts are said to have been witnessed; a male presence is thought to reside in the bedrooms where harsh cold blasts of air have been felt along with tapping on the bedroom doors; light anomalies have also been recorded on camera in this area and a dark shadow has been seen in the corner of one of the rooms.

Worrisome Wooded Areas

When going down to the woods today, be sure to be alert. For lurking in between the trees there could well be more than just the local wildlife ...

HERMIT'S WOOD, ILKESTON, DERBYSHIRE

There is an area of ancient woodland in Ilkeston in Derbyshire called Hermit's Wood which probably formed part of the original forest that once covered this area. It contains many fine beech, oak and lime trees and abundant wildlife but is also home to some strange unexplainable paranormal phenomena: when walking through the trees people have been known to hear strange unexplainable banging noises; sometimes a heavy oppressive atmosphere is said to wash over unsuspecting walkers; and an uneasy feeling of being

159

watched is often felt. Could it be that some unknown force dwells within Hermit's Wood?

There is an old stone archway in the wood, carved out of a sandstone cliff, that forms the entrance to a hermit's cave. It is said that a monk, possibly from the nearby Dale Abbey, committed suicide by hanging himself there and reputedly his apparition has been seen haunting this location.

A Railway Line, Charnwood Forest, Leicestershire

One summer's evening a lady was walking her dog down by an old railway line in one of the woodland areas of Charnwood Forest, when she and her dog got the fright of their lives. As they walked along towards a bridge on the railway line there was a sudden almighty whoosh of air that almost knocked them both off their feet. The woman described this experience as the same kind of feeling you get standing on a railway platform when a train goes through at a great speed. Her hair blew back and all of the hairs on the dog stood up on end. The poor little thing was so petrified that it ran away from its owner and went straight back to her car. Terrified by what had happened that day, it refused to walk down that same path ever again.

After telling her friends at work about he[r] experience, the local postman heard abo[ut] happened to her. Postmen often know a l[ot] has been going on in their area and he was a[ble] the woman in on a macabre event that had taken place on the railway bridge some years before. Apparently a man who could no longer cope with life had tragically committed suicide by throwing himself off the bridge in front of a passing train. Strange things had been known to happen in that area ever since his death.

At 6 pm on that glorious English summer's evening was it the man who committed suicide's final moments that the woman experienced when the gust of wind shook her entire body? Was his ghost returning to the spot where his life ended?

Whatever the reason, it scared the lady and her dog so much that neither of them ever forgot what had happened to them on the old railway line in Charnwood Forest.

WYCHWOOD FOREST, OXFORDSHIRE

Wychwood Forest in Oxfordshire dates back to before medieval times but the forest of today is not anywhere near as vast as it once was many centuries ago. Over the years, many of its trees have had to make way for farmlands, villages and towns. There has been a period of replanting in recent years by the Woodland Trust.

In the mid-1600s, because of the good quality of the trees, they were reserved for use by the Royal Navy. Around five hundred trees were used to build Lord Nelson's flagship, HMS *Victory*.

Aside from its maritime links, the woodland that still remains is also known as a place of paranormal activity: it is said that the sensations of being watched or followed are felt by many when walking through the woods; some say they have had the chilling experience of being touched by an unknown force, while feelings of nausea have been felt by many; others say they have sensed the presence of men riding around on horses in the woodland; and the clip-clopping of hooves in the dead of night on the road nearby is said to have been heard on occasion.

A tree in the forest that is thought to have been used to hang wrongdoers is said to exude otherworldly energies and a male presence has been felt around it. Is this the soul of a hanged man who continues to stay close to the spot where he took his final breath?

Some people also claim to have witnessed the apparition of a man on a horse and cart travelling through the woods, with two crying children sitting in the back of the cart. Whoever they may be, their presence would surely fill anyone who saw this spectacle with dread and fear.

DELAMERE FOREST, CHESHIRE

Delamere Forest is the largest wooded area in Cheshire and draws people to it who wish to enjoy a ramble in the great outdoors. The space that surrounds the forest is said to hold beings from the spirit world.

One night as a car was travelling down a country lane in the forest, a middle-aged lady is said to have appeared in the middle of the road and begun to dance. The driver slowed down and his car came to a halt. He asked the lady if she was alright but received no response. Instead she simply smiled and continued dancing down the road. The lady is said to have been dressed in the sort of clothes worn by women during the Second World War but why her apparition was in Delamere Forest is a mystery. The apparition of this lady has been seen many times and was first reported back in the 1960s.

CLAPHAM WOOD, WEST SUSSEX

Clapham Wood, in the village of Clapham in West Sussex, is well known for being a place where unusual and mysterious events occur.

Along with many tales of UFOs (there are many sightings of unknown lights), this stretch of strange woodland is home to a lot of paranormal activity which may account for a distinct lack of wildlife in the area.

People out for leisurely strolls in the wooded enclave have felt themselves being pushed and pulled in different directions by unknown forces and the feeling of being followed has been well documented over the years. Others have noted feeling sick in the wood when they were not ill in any other way. Could the grey mists which have been sighted on the paths within Clapham Wood hold the key as to why all these strange things have been happening? Is this area haunted by the spirit of a former Clapham resident or the ghost of a person who possibly died in the wood?

Whatever the reasons behind these strange happenings it is easy to see why many people fear going into the wood in the dead of night or even during the day!

CHURSTON WOODS, DEVON

Torbay in Devon is home to a stretch of woodland dating back over four hundred years that is thought to hold ghostly beings. The most famous 'being' to be seen in Churston Woods is said to be a mysterious green monkey creature that is well known in local folklore.

At around 5 feet in height, the creature is far bigger than a normal monkey and is said to have a green face. People have questioned whether this is possibly a bigfoot monster or a spirit manifestation. Whatever it is, the figure has been witnessed many times running through the woods and swinging from tree to tree.

One spooky occurrence that may or may not have involved the green monkey creature happened a few years ago. A small group of people were camping in the nearby disused Seven Quarries. They were enjoying their time in the great outdoors until nightfall approached. Once darkness had fallen the area's atmosphere suddenly changed and the group became edgy and nervous where before they had felt happy and relaxed. They knew no-one had followed them to where they pitched their tent because there was only one way in and out.

After a couple of hours in complete darkness, the terrified group heard footsteps slowly walking around their tent, followed by the sound of heavy breathing. Something strange is then said to have kicked at the ground sheet of the tent making it crease inwards. Scared stiff, the group did not dare to leave until the sun rose and light seeped into their tent.

Bizarre flashes of red light darting around frantically amongst the trees and unexplainable grey wisps of matter floating around the area, similar in appearance to fog, have also been seen. Could all of this be put down to the spirit of an unfortunate soul still wandering Churston Woods in death?

Petrifying Parkland

Breathing fresh air in wide open spaces is a tonic for most, but you could well be walking around with a plethora of dead souls ...

Bradgate Park, Newtown Linford, Leicestershire

Bradgate Park is a public park northwest of Leicester. It covers 850 acres and provides a haven of small woods, grassy slopes and rocky outcrops for ramblers, cyclists and families out for walks. The ruins of Bradgate Hall, once home to Lady Jane Grey, stand within this piece of beautiful countryside. The tragic figure of Lady Jane Grey has fascinated people over many centuries. She was beheaded at the age of sixteen on 12 February 1554 at the Tower of London, only nine days after coming to the throne as Queen of England.

Although pleasant in the heat of summer, the grounds of Bradgate Hall are reputed to become eerily chilling in the depths of winter. The sound of terrifying screams is said to have been heard in the dense bracken around the ruined hall. People claim to have seen a horse-drawn coach gliding around the grounds with a headless ghost, thought to be Lady Jane Grey, sitting inside.

The young Queen suffered a truly horrifying last day on this earth: before being taken to her own death she watched out of a window in the Tower of London as her distraught, sobbing husband, Lord Guildford, was executed. It is said that on the anniversary of her death, the white shimmering ghost of Lady Jane Grey can be seen along the Tower battlements and around the spot where she was executed.

St. James's Park, London

London, one of the premier cities of the world, is well known for the green expanses situated within its boundaries. The oldest of the royal parks is St. James's Park in Westminster, which dates from 1536. Over the centuries many celebrations and happy occasions will undoubtedly have taken place on its grassy carpet but more macabre events have led to the park being known as a haunted spot.

The manifestation of a headless woman dressed in red has often been spotted floating around the park. It is

167

believed that she was killed by her army officer husband who was caught in the act of disposing of her mutilated remains in St. James Park. The apparition of the lady in red has been seen on many different occasions over the last two hundred years and is well documented. A headless monk is also said to dwell within the park but the reason for his presence is a mystery.

On a night-time walk in St. James's Park it may not be just dog-walkers and joggers that cross your path.

Watery Ends

What lies beneath the surface is rarely ever seen but if it ever rises, people will run and scream ...

TALKIN TARN, CUMBRIA

The Talkin Tarn is a lake in the Talkin Tarn Country Park in Cumbria. It lies two miles east of the small market town of Brampton and covers some 60 acres of land. Around the shores of Talkin Tarn, people are said to have borne witness to a startling level of paranormal activity. Many strange lights have been sighted in the dense woodland surrounding the lake and the sound of phantom horses galloping around the area has been heard in the dead of night.

The most famous sighting of ghostly activity took place in 2002 when twenty-three people witnessed a truly mystifying sight. The bloody apparition of a woman is said to have risen from the murky depths of the lake in broad daylight. It is believed that this gruesome vision was possibly the ghost of a lady named Jessie who died in the 1850s by the lake.

Jessie was in love with a rich man and wanted to tell his mother of their love but she did not know that the man was already engaged to a wealthy landowner's daughter. He did not want anything to jeopardise his forthcoming nuptials so he was anxious to keep their affair a secret. Fully believing that her lover felt the same way as she did, Jessie was determined to make their relationship public, much to his annoyance. He offered her money to keep her quiet but Jessie did not want their relationship to be a secret any longer and rejected his offer. Perturbed, the man took her to the lakeside where unbeknownst to Jessie they lay as lovers for the last time. Then he held her head under the lake's water and drowned her, ensuring that Jessie took the knowledge of their clandestine relationship to the grave. He is believed to have placed her body in three sacks and buried it near the water's edge. Jessie's body has never been found but local legend suggests that it is her apparition that has been seen walking hauntingly out of Talkin Tarn's water.

Another legend surrounding the lake is that an entire village was flooded and now sits submerged under the water. The sound of a bell has been heard ringing around midnight, resonating from below the water.

Slapton Sands, Devon

Slapton Sands is a three-mile-long shingle beach on the south coast of Devon. It is most famous for being the beach where Exercise Tiger a beach-landing training exercise during the Second World War, went horribly wrong on 28 April 1944. Many hundreds of American servicemen lost their lives during this training mission, drowning in the cold waters of Lyme Bay as their vessels were caught unawares and torpedoed by German E-boats.

There have been reports of strange sounds resonating from the beach and people have noted hearing the crunching sound of someone walking on the shingle when no-one is to be seen. Unexplainable lights have also been witnessed around this area. These occurrences are said to be more prevalent on the anniversary of Exercise Tiger.

Eerie Entertainment Venues

Laughter and cheer over many a year, but with the passing of time something spooky may this way come ...

A Cinema, King's Cross, London

Ghosts are said to dwell in an old cinema in London's King's Cross who have been mistaken for the living. The cinema, built in the 1930s, was close to King's Cross railway station and back in the 1970s it showed the latest films and housed a dance floor, where regular all-night reggae sessions were held. These gigs would attract reggae fans from far and wide, with well-known performers gracing the stage. However, it is said that it was not only revellers and film fans that graced the building after dark. The spirits of long-dead individuals were also thought to be present!

One night, a manager of the cinema was walking towards his seat after the screening of a film had already begun. It was dark, and rather than looking where he was going, his eyes were fixed on the film on the big screen. Reaching his seat, he put out his hand to steady himself before he sat down. However, to his disbelief it was not the back of the seat that his hand came to rest on but a woman's shoulder, dressed in woolly clothing. Somewhat shocked and embarrassed the man bent down to apologise to the lady, only to find that no-one was there. Could this be the spirit of a lady linked to the locality where the cinema stands?

Whoever she was she clearly has an affinity with the cinema, one that she was not ready to relinquish even in death.

THE GAUMONT THEATRE, LIVERPOOL

In the Toxteth area of Liverpool there is a dilapidated Art Deco building that is said to house benevolent spirits from a time long gone by. The building, which has been a theatre, a cinema and more latterly a bingo hall, stands empty today. Graffiti covers the walls of the once happy place where people used to go to watch a film, dance the night away at a music gig or play bingo. Laughter and good cheer would often have reverberated throughout the building.

However, it is only the haunting sounds of dead

173

souls that fills the building today. Now run-down and derelict, the Gaumont's interior lies in a terrible state with broken furniture and decaying rubbish strewn all over the floor. The droppings of the pigeons that have made the former cinema their home cover everything. There is no doubt that for anyone visiting the Gaumont after dark, the sounds of broken glass being crunched underfoot and the cooing of the pigeons all serve to heighten the building's eerie and oppressive atmosphere and people are terrified to be left alone in any part of it.

The paranormal activity experienced within the old theatre has scared the living daylights out of many unsuspecting visitors. People claim to have seen a number of manifestations of men and women haunting the building while strange lights and looming shadowy figures are said to have been witnessed frequently, sending fear through any person unfortunate enough to come into contact with them.

Could any of these happenings be the result of the rumoured suicide of a man who is thought to have hung himself behind the old cinema screen?

Local legend also suggests that a lady died whilst playing bingo in the Gaumont – her heart no longer able to take the excitement of the game. It is believed by many that her ghost still lurks in the shadows of the old Art Deco building, trapped where she met her untimely end.

Anyone who enters the old theatre today most certainly does so at their own risk. For at any moment they could quite possibly come face to face with some of the sinister spirits that float around the walls and floors of the once grand Gaumont Theatre.

⊙∽⤞∻⤝∾⊙

The Falstaff Experience, 40 Sheep Street, Stratford upon Avon, Warwickshire

Visitors from all around the world are drawn in their thousands to the town of Shakespeare's birth, Stratford upon Avon. During the day the streets buzz with happy tourists, eager to indulge in the work and life of the Bard.

However, long before William Shakespeare graced the town, a building stood at the now spooky 40 Sheep Street. Over the centuries the structure has had a few re-incarnations but the building that stands today consists of a wattle-and daub house and a large 16th century barn. For the past 500 years this structure has been known as Shrieves House, after the first known tenant of the building William Shrieve, who lived there from 1536 and was a noble archer to King Henry VIII during his rein over England.

In the 16th century the property became the Three Tunns Tavern and the tavern keeper, William Rogers, is thought to have been the inspiration for Shakespeare's famous comic character, Falstaff.

Along with William Shakespeare there have been other famous historical figures who have graced the premises. These have reportedly included Oliver

Cromwell, who is said to have stayed in the building before the Battle of Worcester during the English Civil War.

With a building as old as 40 Sheep Street it is not surprising to find that it is thought to house many spirits. Both staff and visitors to the Falstaff Experience at 40 Sheep Street have reported paranormal occurrences on a daily basis. There are said to be a number of dominant ghoulish spirits that haunt this property, including a serial murderer from the 18th century, the archer William Shrieves and a poor little girl who was a pickpocket in the tavern, a Catholic gentleman from the time of the reformation and a justice of the peace who reputedly used his power to run an extortion ring with threats, violence and trumped-up charges from within the old tavern.

People also claim to have seen the figures of Parliamentarian soldiers and some have even felt the injuries suffered by the unfortunate soldiers during a battle that took place nearby. It is also said that the spirits of many children and animals roam within the walls of the old building and on occasion people have witnessed a menacing figure with evil red glowing eyes watching from darkened corners within the building.

Ruined Roman Remains

They came, conquered and helped to form the country we call England today ...

CHESTER WALLS

The Roman town of Chester has a long history of paranormal tales and otherworldly goings-on. With so many old buildings and with such a rich history it is easy to see why.

Walls surround the city and it is here that many people have witnessed something that can only be put down to paranormal activity: they have seen the figure of a Roman soldier wandering with his general in the vicinity of Northgate Street. It would appear that these spirits are still staunchly carrying out their military duties and defending Chester from attack.

It is widely believed that the original Roman

settlement lies beneath modern-day Chester. This could be the reason for the plethora of apparent hauntings linked to the time when the city was one of Rome's biggest British garrison towns.

⌒⤜⧓⤛⌒

CAWTHORN ROMAN CAMPS, NORTH YORKSHIRE

Some 2,000 years ago England was soon to be in the grip of the Roman Empire and what was to come shaped the nation as we know it today. A hundred years or so later, in deepest darkest North Yorkshire the Romans were expanding their military empire. In the central moorlands of what is now North York National Park they built three fortifications as part of a military complex – two forts and a temporary marching camp. Later, after the Romans had departed the Vikings are believed to have taken ownership of the area.

Many people are said to have witnessed paranormal activity around the Cawthorn Camps. Undoubtedly there would have been hundreds of people living at one time within the area, going about their daily chores and training for battle. Some would have died in and around the Cawthorn Camps, whether through ill health, during training, or inevitably during disputes that possibly led to murder.

A multitude of mysterious flashing lights have been seen whizzing around the place where the Camps once stood. Are these the souls of Roman soldiers long departed but still roaming the land where they once worked and lived? They could also be connected to the imposing sound of marching, which has been heard around the area.

Mysteriously however, the figure of a modern-day man has been seen wandering around the perimeter of the Camps. On one occasion a group of people saw the same man in some trees nearby. Intrigued, they wandered closer to where he stood when to their astonishment a man's voice shouted out 'Hello' before the apparition vanished. At the time of this spooky happening there were no other living people present in the area.

SILCHESTER ROMAN TOWN, HAMPSHIRE

The Roman town at Silchester was abandoned back in the 5th century, but before its decline into ruin it was abuzz with life. Silchester was founded as part of the Roman Empire and given the name Calleva Atrebatum by its occupiers. Since the days of its abandonment the ground on which it stood has not been built over, making the site an archaeologist's dream. Many digs have been performed on the site and because of this many facts are known about the ancient Roman town that once stood there.

Excavations at the site have brought to life many of the buildings that once formed the old Roman town and the amphitheatre is one such structure. Within this area spectators would have watched as animals and humans butchered each other in the name of both entertainment and punishment. With so much brutality and death, the amphitheatre is sure to hold spirits who are yet to leave this ancient space. Some witnesses claim to have seen unexplainable white lights around this area and the smell of new leather is sometimes present. The reason for this smell could be paranormal as leather was one of the most popular types of material worn by the Romans, in particular in battle and when fighting as gladiators.

A Mixture of Manifestations

There are ghostly manifestations lurking in all sorts of places ...

COALHOUSE FORT, EAST TILBURY, ESSEX

In green parkland next to the River Thames in East Tilbury, there sits a magnificant Victorian coastal defence fort called Coalhouse Fort. Since 1874 the structure has waited for attack from France and its fellow European mainland countriesand it continued to serve as a defence through the last two World Wars but was then sold off. It now sits redundant and empty. However the fort is not as unlived in as it would appear from the outside, because it is believed that dead souls are still present inside.

Throughout its time as a military garrison there would have been many people living, working and sleeping within this defensive stronghold. The fort is said to have an electric atmosphere, charged by the paranormal forces at work within. Many dark eerie tunnels form part of Coalhouse Fort and anyone entering them is said to experience great fear. Audible phenomena are prevalent within the fort and are the most common form of paranormal activity found there: loud, frightening footsteps from an unknown entity echo around the tunnels and are said to sound as if they are walking towards people before suddenly stopping; other strange sounds are often heard within Coalhouse Fort, including banging and rapping on the walls. Where these noises come from, no-one can pinpoint, but they are certainly not made by anything living.

Using an infrared light on one occasion, breath was seen to show up but who or what it was coming from is not known. Seemingly there are also dramatic temperature fluctuations all around the fort that are not triggered by any natural force. Apparitions of ghostly men have also been seen wandering this haunted fort.

SELWYN HOUSE PREP SCHOOL, ST. PETER'S ROAD, BROADSTAIRS, KENT

Down on the south-east coast of England the coastal county of Kent has been widely regarded as the Garden of England for 400 years thanks to its orchards, farmland and beautiful countryside. But take a walk away from the beautiful scenery and stunning shoreline and you will find an old boarding school that is said to have housed many spirits.

A former pupil of the school has recounted how early one morning at around 6.30 am he awoke in his dormitory. It was light and his roommates were chattering away with excitement. Unable to sleep any longer he rose from his bed to see what was happening. To his amazement he saw that on one of the boy's beds there sat the shape of a hunched-over forlorn figure. Startled by what he was seeing the boy stared in amazement. The apparent manifestation did not say a word and after about five minutes slowly faded away in front of his eyes.

It seems that the ghost witnessed by the dormitory of boys had been seen by many other pupils over the years and it had even been given a name. The ghost was called Bunkum after some pupils reported what they had seen to the headmaster and he is said to have exclaimed, 'Oh, that's bunkum!' as if trying to brush the matter aside. What the boys witnessed that morning will surely have stayed in the minds of many and one wonders if Bunkum still wanders that space today?

Another story connected to the former boarding school originates during the Second World War, when it was used as a hospital for injured soldiers. It is reported that for some reason a pilot ejected from his plane and parachuted down onto the roof of one of the dormitories. The propeller of the pilot's wrecked plane took pride of place in the school for many years after and it is said that every year since then in the middle of the night the sound of something sliding down the roof can sometimes be heard.

Winter's Gibbet, Elsdon, Northumberland

A gibbet is a large wooden structure from which the dead bodies of executed criminals were hung on public display. After execution their remains would be placed in chains or in a metal cage and hung from the gibbet in full view of people with the intention of deterring others from committing similar crimes. It is believed that some people were also placed in cages when they were still alive and left to die an agonising death.

Winter's Gibbet, or Elsdon Gibbet as it is also known, is a macabre memorial to crime that stands near a small medieval village in the north-east of England named Elsdon. The structure was named after William Winter who planned and committed a despicable and cowardly crime with accomplices Jane and Eleanor Clark. One dreadful day back in 1792 the evil trio broke into the home of a defenceless old lady named Mary Crozier and proceeded to rob and kill their helpless victim.

The evil trio were caught and found guilty and all were executed for their terrible wrongdoings. William Winter was hung in Newcastle and his body returned to where he had carried out his dastardly plan. The bodies of the Clark sisters were given to local doctors to be dissected. William's body hung in a gibbet's cage while birds, flies and maggots sickeningly ate away at his eyeballs and the flesh on his corpse. Eventually nothing remained of the villain apart from his bones which were then scattered.

The gibbet as it now stands is not the original one but was erected during the 1860s. However, according to a plaque on the gibbet, it stands on the spot where the original structure stood and there is said to be paranormal activity on a substantial scale all around.

The figure of a man thought to be William Winter has been spotted frequently in the area and is said to often walk near a cattle grid there. Dark shadows have been witnessed around the gibbet. Could these be the spirits of long-dead criminals, gracing the spot with their presence where once their dead bodies hung?

People claim to have seen strange lights around this part of the countryside coming from no apparent source. Terrifying bloodcurdling screams have also been heard in the area sending fear through anyone who hears them. Who or what is generating them is not known.

Being in the area around Winter's Gibbet could scare even the most sceptical of people and it continues to be an intriguing location for anyone interested in the paranormal.

THE SPANISH BARN, TORQUAY

In the seaside town of Torquay there is an old stone barn that dates back many hundreds of years. The Spanish Barn, as it is known, is a Grade-I listed building originally built in 1196 by the canons of Torre Abbey. It was used as a tithe barn for the abbey, where taxes paid in the form of farm produce were stored. In 1450 the barn that we see today had its roof put on a few hundred years after it was first constructed. Its unusual name came about after a galleon that was part of the Spanish Armada was captured nearby. The three hundred and ninety-seven members of the stricken *Nuestra Senora del Rosario* were brought to the barn by locals and imprisoned there for two weeks, after which they were moved to prisons in Dartmouth and Exeter.

Although the barn that stands today is a perfectly pleasant place to visit, it is said to house some strange paranormal activity including a stench of decay and disease that can wash over a person in an instant but has no known source. The barn's most famous ghost is known as 'the Spanish Lady'. She is believed to have died in the Spanish Barn after disguising herself as a man so that she could be with her fiancé when he was imprisoned there with the other members of the *Rosario*'s crew. Sadly she died there and it is said that her ghost, weeping for her lost love, still likes to roam the barn and the surrounding parkland.

CRAG HALL MINE, CARLIN HOW, YORKSHIRE

There is an old ironstone mine in Yorkshire that is said to be the site of a macabre murder, which took place on Christmas Eve back in 1873. A group of young labourers (who were eventually brought to justice) beat up the tragic victim, a woman named Mary Ward, and threw her down a mine shaft. Her ghost is said to haunt the area and since she met her unfortunate end people claim to have seen her on a number of occasions in the nearby villages of Carlin How and Skinningrove.

In Carlin How she is believed to visit the Maynard Arms pub. Once a customer of the pub, her ghost is said to walk the path between it and the spot where she was murdered.

In the village of Skinningrove, Mary's manifestation has been seen near the old ironstone mine. Just before she was murdered she had been out wassailing, going from house to house with a little box containing a statue of the Virgin Mary in the hope that her singing would result in the gift of some money or food. Her ghost is said to carry the little box even in death.

CALLOW HILL, HEREFORDSHIRE

There once stood a coaching inn on Callow Hill in Herefordshire, that is believed to have been a place of murder and deception. Wealthy weary travellers in horse-drawn carriages would stop off to eat, drink and sleep unaware of what was to befall them.

It is said that a small gang of two or three felons would watch for coaches approaching the inn and once all the passengers were inside set about their dastardly plan. They would enter the tavern of the inn and ply one of the well-to-do drinkers with alcohol all evening. As the rest of the guests departed for bed, the lonesome, somewhat intoxicated man or woman would be left alone with the felons. The unfortunate victim would then be murdered and carried out of the inn, across two fields to an abandoned house where their body would be stripped of all valuables and material. Leaving their victim's body at the house, the felons would then return to the inn to empty the victim's room of all belongings. They did this to make it appear that the murdered person had left and continued on his travels ahead of his fellow passengers. They then made sure that everyone was informed of this fake departure the next morning.

The villains carried out this plan many times but eventually people began to get suspicious and criminal investigations were carried out. The gruesome gang were eventually caught and hung for their crimes. When the abandoned house was inspected, the rotting remains of between eighteen and thirty people were discovered. Horrified by this, the local people burnt down the house. Nobody knows for sure where the house stood as nature has seen fit to remove all traces of the building since it was burnt down.

However, it would seem that the house does return to its former location as people travelling through the area claim to have witnessed an apparition of the house appearing in front of them and in some cases have seen two figures dragging what would appear to be a dead body across a field and into the house. Hereford Police have also received countless reports of people witnessing a fire at a building on Callow Hill, even though no such building exists. Could this be some kind of paranormal re-enactment of the burning of the abandoned house? Whatever it is, the term 'haunted' would certainly seem to be appropriate when discussing Callow Hill in Herefordshire.

St. Mary's Guildhall, Coventry, Warwickshire

The West Midlands city of Coventry houses one of the finest examples of a medieval guildhall in England. St. Mary's Guildhall has stood in the centre of Coventry for over 650 years and has been a building of much importance throughout history. It was the base for Henry VI's court during the infamous War of the Roses, in which he fought King Richard III for the crown. Some years later it briefly became a prison for Mary Queen of Scots, during her nineteen years of imprisonment and before she was executed by Elizabeth I in 1567. William Shakespeare, is believed to have staged plays at the Guildhall. During the Second World War Coventry was heavily bombed, but the Guildhall stood firm with only a few scars to its structure.

Coventry Guildhall has staged many banquets over the centuries and welcomed dignataries, noblemen and royalty through its doors. On one occasion an uninvited guest was photographed indulging in the surroundings of the grand building. The photograph shows a mysterious figure standing next to a table during a banquet that took place at the Guildhall. This vision has come to be known as 'the Mystery Guest' and is a famous example of ghostly photography.

Paranormal phenomena are known to be prevalent within the Guildhall, with unexplainable flashes of light and loud bangs reverberating around its interior. These mysterious occurrences are not believed to come from any human activity. Perhaps the Mystery Guest has something to do with them?

A sense of unease is also experienced by unsuspecting visitors to the Guildhall who have felt obscure cold spots within the building. Camera batteries are also known to have suddenly been drained of all their energy inside the Guildhall for no apparent reason.

With a long and full history and many thousands of people passing through its doors, it comes as no surprise that Coventry Guildhall houses some uninvited spooky characters.

Acknowledgements

The author and publishers are very grateful to the following organisations and individuals for permission to include facts and information from their rescarch in this book:

Abbey Ghosthunters at
  www.abbeyghosthunters.co.uk
Arthur C. Howell, *Grove Mill, Canal Mill & Botany Bay*, Tempus Publishing Ltd
Bristol Society For Paranormal Investigation and
  Research at
  www.bspri.org.uk
Cheshire Paranormal at
  www.cheshireparanormal.co.uk

Clitheroe Paranormal at
  www.clitheroeparanormal.com
Colin Crosby, Crosby Heritage at
  www.crosbyheritage.co.uk
Ghost-story.co.uk
Ghosts of the North East (Rob Kirkup)
Natalie Lawrence at Haunted Hereford at
  www.haunted-hereford.co.uk
Hidden Realms Paranormal Investigators
Ken Taylor
Luton Paranormal at
  www.lutonparanormal.com
Manchester Haunted at
  www.manchesterhaunted.com
Paranormal Investigation Group Sussex at
  www.the-pigs.co.uk
Spirit Team UK at
  www.spiritteamuk.com
Supernatural Investigations at
  www.supernaturalinvestigations.org.uk
Thames Valley Paranormal Group at
  www.tvpg.co.uk